HOW TO LIVE

How to Live

Jewish Science Essays

by

Rabbi Morris Lichtenstein

*Leader and Founder of the Society of Jewish Science
Author of the Text-book of Jewish Science,
"Jewish Science and Health,"
"Peace of Mind," etc.*

ॐ

JEWISH SCIENCE PUBLISHING CO.
NEW YORK

DEDICATED

With Blessings to the

SOCIETY OF JEWISH SCIENCE

Whose members are striving
for the realization of the ideal.

CONTENTS

CONTENTS

HOW TO LIVE

LIVING LIFE OVER AGAIN

More often than any other wish, perhaps, do we hear men express the desire to live life over again, to leap back to their youthful years and reincarnate them, to drive back the stream of their days to its incipient flow. Why do we long so avidly to wipe out the past days and years, and start our journey once more at its beginning? For one of two reasons. Either we are conscious of errors and blunders and extravagances committed in youthful unwisdom and are anxious to correct or eradicate our misdoings; or we wish again to enjoy the intense pleasures of youth, to taste again the hilarious and careless mirth of our early days.

Let us address ourselves first to those among us who wish to live life over again in order to correct their past errors. What would living life over again mean? It would mean that a man, say, of sixty or seventy, be rejuvenated into a youth of twenty, it would mean that the wrinkles of maturity be pressed out and re-

placed with the freshness of youth, that the
hair cast off its grayness and resume its original luster and color, that the limbs again regain their past vigor, that the organs and
functions renew their old virility and power,
that the body become charged with its former
energy and vitality.   Let us suppose that all
this has taken place.   What will then follow?
The passions and desires will stir from their
quietude and burst forth again with potency
and energy; selfish cravings, untempered ambitions, negative, destructive schemes will again
charge the heart and overpower the mind.
Thought will then recede, judgment will stand
conquered, and conscience helpless.   And what
will follow?   Man will then commit the very
same blunders which he now regrets, he will act
in the very same manner that has brought him
to his present state of remorse.

You may contend that the desire to live life
over again means a desire to live it over with
youthful years but with mature understanding;
with the vigor and vitality of former days but
with the wisdom and judgment of advanced
age.   This is even more extravagant a fancy
than that of living life over in its normal and

regular state; for it contains a desire not only to alter the process of nature, but to change the very fundamental purpose of existence. With clear vision and ripe judgment and mature wisdom in our unripe years, our individual world would be one of ready-made, premature perfection. Man is born to strive, to struggle with the world and with himself, to bend every effort in his being in order to attain perfection; not to have it prepared for him. Nothing in nature attains perfection without a struggle; the flower must struggle with heat and cold before it attains its full beauty; the tree is constantly in contact with tempest and blight, it is bent and shaken by gale and storm, until it attains the mature strength wherewith it is able to withstand with ease the onslaught of the elements; the stream is exposed to drought and exhaustion until it digs for itself a deep, wide bed wherein to flow. Man too must struggle before he attains wisdom, he must pass through many clouds before he attains clearness of vision; his mature understanding must be the result of experience, his ripeness of judgment must be the prize gained after many lessons in endurance and drudgery. Conscience itself obtains its greatest victories over the individual only after many trials and setbacks.

No! Man need not wish to have back his former days in order to enable himself to correct the errors of his past; he need not long for the years that are dead in order to live life over with better judgment and clearer understanding. He can live life over again from *today* on. A new life may be opened to him at this very hour. Every hour marks a new creation, every day a new existence. Then why long to efface the past? Why not renew life today, even as nature renews itself each day? Rather than correct our past, which is an impossible task and therefore but a fantastic wish, we are privileged to correct our present—a task which is possible and vital.

Man's regret or remorse over his past, marks a rather wholesome progress in his nature. It means that today he is much bigger than he was; that his faculties are finer, that his heart is more warm, that his ideals are more noble, that his conscience is more active, that his outlook upon life is more earnest and more judicious, that he is able to look down from a height upon his former self. But a regret that remains merely a regret misses its purpose. We fail if we only regret; we gain if our regret brings about definite transformations in our being, if it leads us on to a finer life, if it serves as an urgent, driving power, impelling us in the direction of greater perfection, if it leads us, not to wish back our former days, but to begin life over. And this we can do at once. If our past years have been spent in idleness and indolence, let us begin today to live a life of industry and achievement, a life of purposive action and constructive accomplishment. If our past days have been marked with ignorance, we can still today learn and acquire knowledge. It is never too late to inform ourselves of the world in which we dwell; it is never too late to comprehend more clearly and minutely that which others and ourselves witness about us and experience every day. Knowledge is not confined to school days; it is the requirement of every day of our life. If our past was marked by cold-heartedness, by uncharitableness or unkindness, we can start today to live a life of sympathy, of openheartedness, of tenderness; we can unlock the confines of our heart and release the emotions of love and benevolence that have been imprisoned there. We can force our hand to relax its niggardliness, and in its stead pour forth its generosity and charity. If our past has been filled with excesses and indulgences and extravagances, again we can correct these errors by beginning today a life of purity and moderation and self-control. There is nothing in our past that we cannot rectify in the present, if we are willing to begin life over with greatness of spirit and fineness of conscience.

To those among us who wish to live life over, not in order to correct past errors, but in order to relive past joys, we would say it is erroneous to think that joy is confined to youth, or even that our greatest, deepest joys are experienced in our days of youth. Every stage, every season of our existence has its own joys, even as every stage of nature, every season in nature, has its own beauty and glory. Childhood has its joys, youth its joys, maturity its joys, and advanced age, too, has its joys. Joy in childhood is gained through toy and game; joy in youth through the stirring of ambition and the winning of love; in maturity, joy is found through achievement and through a perfect home life; in advanced age, joy comes with a clearer comprehension of the meaning of life, with the realization of the true and noble significance of existence, with the devotion to and identification of the self with the welfare of humanity. It would be the acme of absurdity for a youth to seek to go back to his childhood days in order to enjoy again his dolls and his blocks and his fairy tales. It is equally absurd for mature manhood to desire the joys which unripe, inexperienced youth had once yielded. Our joys follow the advancement of our understanding. The higher our judgment, the more mature our wisdom, the clearer our vision, the higher must be the source which furnishes us joy. And it is for this very reason that the joys of youth differ greatly from the joys of maturity. The joys of youth come in the form of pleasure, while the joys of maturity come in the form of happiness. And there is a clear distinction between pleasure and happiness. Pleasure is the satisfaction of the body, happiness is the satisfaction of the soul; pleasure is therefore temporary, for the body is always in a changeable state, while happiness is permanent; for the soul is immutable.

Pleasure has the brightness of lightning, while happiness has the brightness of sunshine. Pleasure is a single sound, happiness is a symphony. Pleasure may frequently have the disapproval of conscience, happiness never. The one is experienced chiefly in the days of passion and immaturity, the other accompanies the days of serenity and wisdom.

To experience joy, one need not live life over again, for the very stage at which one is has joys greater than the ones longed for. Do you but direct your vision upon your present, instead of upon your past, and you will soon discover countless sources which may yield you happiness. To long for the past is only another way of running away from the joys of the present. Open but your eyes, and see the endless sources of joy *today* before you. To do *something,* and to do it well, is a source of happiness. A great deal of unhappiness can be traced to a passage through life without occupation and without purpose. Man is endowed with definite energies, with definite capacities; when these find an outlet in constructive, creative action, he becomes filled with joy, just as, on the other hand, if he fritters and idles away his days, he becomes filled with discontent and depression. And just as it is a source of joy to give expression to one's creative energies, so is it also an inexhaustible source of happiness to give expression to one's finer emotions. To bring into action earnest sympathy, to identify oneself with the needs of others, to lift up those who have stumbled, to cheer those who are unfortunate, to encourage those who are disheartened, to share with others any spiritual blessings that we may possess, all these are inexhaustible sources of happiness. Likewise, the promotion of an ideal, the unselfish service and self-sacrifice which one renders for the advancement of that ideal, will unfailingly bring abundant measures of happiness. One need not become metamorphosed back into an uncultivated, unripe youth in order to gain joy; one can, in maturity, attain much deeper, much finer joys, joys that satisfy the heart and ennoble the mind.

To desire to live life over again is essentially a desire to improve oneself, to obtain more from life, to lift oneself from conscious shortcomings and to gain more joy. But to attain these, one need not literally live over the days that are past; one need only reform today what he would have reformed, gain today what he would have gained, live today as he would have lived if he could live life over again.

MASTERING OUR NERVES

Man is born to be a master. A master, but not necessarily a ruler. The ruler seeks to subordinate, to subdue those whom he rules, to impose his will and his judgment upon others. The master endeavors to gain a clearer and deeper understanding of the nature of that object or circumstance or sphere which he seeks to master. His interest is in the object, not necessarily in himself. He too seeks to control, but not in order to dominate; in order, rather, to guide and direct. The ruler seeks dominion, the master seeks knowledge.

Man is born to be a master—he is born to master his environment, to master his task, to master himself; he is born to mould and fashion the circumstances in which he is placed, to gain a deeper and still deeper understanding of the sphere in which his energies are active, and to direct, with increasing control and perfection, his own emotions and actions. This last form of mastery is the greatest of all; in fact, the direction and control of all the other fields of attainment are dependent upon this one. When one has learned to master himself, when he has learned to control his inner world, it becomes easy for him to control his outer world. When he is able to harness his will to his judgment, his active powers to his creative visions, his desires to his conscience, it becomes comparatively easy for him to master his environment and obtain from it that which is useful and salutary and elevating. If he succeeds in uprooting unwholesome tendencies from his inner being, he will prove even more victorious, and with less effort, in his combat with the difficulties which he may encounter in his outer world. For self-mastery is the keynote to life mastery, and self-control is the road that leads to the control of the world around us.

But while we speak of the mastery of the self, we are well aware that the self is not at all a simple entity, that it does not consist of a unitary element which can easily be released or easily restrained, but that it is a composite of multifarious inclinations, many of which are native and many acquired, many of which are wholesome and many injurious, many of which should be encouraged and given free expression and many discouraged and checked. It is our purpose here to indicate how we may beneficially direct and control that phase of the self which, in men and women of our generation, is dangerously weak—we refer to the *nervous self*.

Our generation is rich in progress, rich in possessions, rich in comfort, rich in knowledge, but it is poor in health, poor in strength, poor in quietude and in peace of mind. This is because we are extremists in our desires, in our efforts and in our struggles. We pound away our energy as if we were of inexhaustible stuff. We drive our limbs urgently and recklessly, we impel our bodies into constant and breathless action; we throw our hearts out of rhythm and balance, we goad our nervous system to exhaustion. Our natural self, our serene self, our divine self, we mutilate and transform into a restless, rushing, disquiet thing. Watch men on the busy streets, observe them in the market-place, note how hectic their action, how disturbed their motion, how impatient their gestures, how tense and straining their faces, how rapid their speech. They act with all

that they possess, desperately, almost trag-
ically, not caring apparently what is left in
them for the next day. This extreme manner
of acting and living, this continuous wastage
of energy and power is the outstanding weakness of our generation, and the cause of the
restlessness and nervousness prevalent to-day.

Our nervous system is subject to training.
We train our nerves just as we train our
muscles; we train our manner and our rhythm
of action just as we train our senses and our
faculties; we give our nervous system a method
of living just as we give our minds information and knowledge. And just as our mind
retains the knowledge that we have stored away
in it, especially when that is often refreshed,
so do our nerves follow the method of action
impressed upon them, particularly when that is
daily repeated. If we train our nervous system
to make haste, it will quickly learn the lesson
of making haste. It will resist the will, it will
not follow the dictates of judgment, it will
simply make haste, and it will learn that lesson
better and better, making haste whether haste
be called for or not. Therefore those who
hurry, *always* hurry. They hurry throughout

their business hours, they hurry through their meal hours, they hurry in their social hours, they hurry in their leisure hours. They are always in a hurry. They are like a raft in a storm that is unable to halt its course, they are like a mechanism that is wound up and cannot stop itself. There is nothing to demand it, and yet the limbs continue their racing, the heart continues its leaping, the mind its impatient swing, until all the energies become overstrained, the vitality is exhausted, and the individual falls into a state of continued fatigue. The reservoir of his nervous energy having become depleted, he ceases to rush, but only because he has become incapable of so doing; his nervous system has given way, and a breakdown has resulted.

But there is no reason why rational, intelligent human beings should not foresee the danger that lies before them, there is no reason why they should foster habits which cause nervous exhaustion and suffering, why they should violate their own nature and live a life of tension and rush. Call a halt to this mad way of living! Slow down! Command your limbs to stop their racing, command your body to stop its rushing, command your energies to cease their wasteful outpourings, and you will regain yourself; you will become again master of yourself. Re-train your nervous system; just as it has exaggerated hitherto its strain and rush, so must you now in order to bring it back to its normal self, compel it to exaggerate in slowness and ease. Re-train your nervous system; set it back, force it back to its serene state. Force back the energies, which have been wastefully poured forth, into the reservoir within. Put a stop to the outflowing streams of strength; put a stop to the ceaseless consumption of vitality and power; let these assert themselves only when called upon for vital achievement and creation. Have constantly before you these two words: *"Be serene."* See them with your mental eye wherever you are and whatever you may be doing. Be serene in your work. When at your desk many interests may be claiming your attention, lend your attention serenely; write, dictate, give orders, receive directions calmly. Receive even unpleasant news, listen even to unpleasant words, serenely. Take in all that life has to offer, not with an indifferent, but with a serene mind. It is not so difficult a task as it may at first appear. Your hasty, nervous self is not your natural self, it is an acquired self; it is your sickly self. Your serene self is your natural self, it is your healthy self. It is easier far to live one's natural life than to live the role of an acquired self. With serenity always before you as your object, you will, you must, succeed in regaining yourself. You will not only transform yourself but you will also create a healthy, serene atmosphere about you, which will be sensed by and influence all those who have contact with you.

Just as our nerves, if so stimulated, are apt to run recklessly onward, so are they also apt to run downward. Just as they can acquire a state of tension and haste, so can they also develop a state of depression and unhappiness. Nerves may be trained to feel miserable, just as they may be trained to be wasteful. Not all those who complain of unhappiness have cause to be unhappy; not all those who are morose have reason for their melancholy. It is often but the illusion of our ill-trained nerves. We have steeped them too often in a gloomy atmosphere, have shown them too often a gloomy outlook, and now they persist in seeing gloom everywhere. At first we lead them, and then they lead us. When the nerves take a downward swoop, we can see nothing but unhappiness in life. We can see no hope, no cheer, no sun. Our bodies may be strong and vigorous, our minds healthy and keen, but some lowering clouds have made their abode in our being, and they veil from our vision the light of the world. Every phase of life, therefore, every circumstance, every color, is dark and unhappy.

Here, too, the individual can himself tear away the veil of unhappiness from his vision. Here, too, he can change his horizon. He can re-train his nerves. He can make a conscious effort and a strong effort to reset his mind into its natural joyful state. Let him refuse to speak depressing words, though he may be experiencing depressing thoughts; let him force his lips to smile, even when his heart is heavy; let him force himself to walk out in the sunshine, to receive the fresh and penetrating glow of God's light and air, even though he may desire to immure himself withindoors; let him read cheerful books, hear cheerful music, seek the company of cheerful folk. His mind will then in time refill with cheerful thought, his heart will be recharged with cheerful feeling, he will find himself performing cheer-giving acts; he will have regained himself, he will have again become master of himself.

You may be prompted to ask: in this conscious process of re-training and remastering our nerves, what application may be made of the power of prayer? Let me say that a prayer should not be offered when the individual persists wilfully in violating the divine law of his nature. A prayer is most effective when the individual himself shows a desire to be helped. When the individual desists from his pernicious habits, when he makes a conscious effort to help himself, then this effort is in itself a prayer. When the individual takes no step, cares not, wills not to eradicate that which is ruinous to his life, then the Divine Mind too is silent, and help fails to come. An effort for self-correction is a prayer, an effort for self-direction is a prayer, an effort for self-elevation, self-restitution is a prayer, and these prayers are always answered.

PROLONGING THE SPAN OF LIFE

As soon as man discovered that there is no
uniformity in the span of life, that some men,
in other words, live longer than others, that
life can be lengthened under favorable circumstances and shortened under unfavorable
circumstances, he set out to find a means by
which the duration of his life might be prolonged. And in each age or generation the
search for such a means was naturally in accord with the understanding of that age. In
the epoch of fancy and superstition, adventur-
ers went out to distant lands in quest of the
fountain of perpetual youth. Fantastic theories
and unbelievable legends surrounded this
chimerical goal, but with the growth, in later
generations, of reason and scientific knowledge, this fantasy melted away. At another
period, the alchemists, who tried to turn base
metal into gold, attempted, with equal assidu-
ity, to find a potion that would prolong human
life indefinitely. They had a better understanding of life and of man than did their prede-

cessors, but their efforts too were vain, for no chemical compound or drug could they find which would magically increase man's years on earth. In very recent years, and to-day also, medical men have been seeking to prolong youth and life by the transfusion of the glandular substances of lower animals into the human system. No notably successful results have been brought forward from these experiments, and the medical profession itself is skeptical of the claims put forward for this method. No physical substance has, to this day, been discovered which has the power of adding years to man's life.

The fallacy in all these efforts lies, we believe, in the fact that all these seekers for prolonged life have taken it for granted that man is essentially a body, and whatever else he may possess are only additions to his body; they have therefore been laboring to preserve this body in its living state—all aiming at the same goal, and all attempting to achieve it through the injection of some material substance into the *body*. But man is not fundamentally a body. The chief essence of his make-up is mind. Mind it is that rules and directs the life of man. Mind it is that sees and interprets, plans and builds, searches and comprehends. Mind it is that rejoices or is afflicted, that experiences happiness or endures suffering, that hopes or is despondent; mind it is that lives and wills and achieves. When the mind ceases to function, the body becomes useless. Man, we repeat, is essentially mind, the body is only an instrument in the hands of the mind, it is a tool wherewith the mind marks out its existence on earth. Therefore when we seek to prolong the span of human life, the starting step must be made, not with the body, but with the mind.

If you are prompted to ask these questions: Is it not the body that grows old and weak and feeble with the advance of years, while the mind it is that grows stronger and more experienced and more clear and accurate in its observation and judgment, as the years advance? Does this not show that the mind reacts in one way and the body in another to the passage of time? We answer that the body was not divinely intended to grow old and feeble with the passing of the years. On the contrary; physiologists will tell you that a process is operating in the body, the chief function of which is to counteract the inroads of age. A process of perpetual renewal is active in the body. The cells of which the body is composed are being constantly replaced and renewed. Some of the cells of our body are renewed every few days, others every few weeks, and still others—particularly the cells which compose the bony structure—every few months. During the period of a single year, all the cells of the body are renewed. In other words, there is not a single cell in our body to-day that was there a year ago. Since the last year, all the tissues, all the substances composing our bodies, have been replaced and renewed. The flesh of our being is not the same to-day as it was in the year that has passed; it is entirely new, although we are not conscious of its renewal. This shows that divine care is taken of our bodies, that they should not of themselves grow infirm and decrepit. The feebleness and infirmity which befall man in his advanced days and shorten his life, is not, we say, due to inherent weakness in the flesh, but to a misuse or misdirection of the mental processes which affect the body directly.

We say that the span of human life can be lengthened, not through arbitrary preservatives applied to the body, but through the proper, wholesome uses of the mind. Our thoughts, our mental habits, can ruin us, as well as preserve us, they can shorten our years as well as multiply them. Our bodies are but active tools to serve our minds, and they are affected by the mind both for health and for suffering, in accordance with its mood and direction.

Let me say, first of all, that in order to prolong the span of life, the mind must not be permitted to think in terms of *end*. Man must not go on suggesting to himself, as the years pass: My face is growing old, my motions are becoming sluggish, my powers are waning, I am losing my hold upon life, I can see the end near. Do not impress it upon your consciousness that because one or both of your parents died at a premature age, therefore your life on earth also cannot be long. Do not speak of death, do not think of death, do not center your mind upon that season when things wither and fade. Do not in your mind associate weakness with sixty, infirmity with seventy, and helplessness with eighty. All these thoughts serve as suggestions to the body and they leave their mark upon the body and its vital processes. We are so constituted that we ourselves can and do influence the span of our lives. Consciously or unconsciously we are constantly talking things into ourselves, and our bodies react constantly to the suggestions given them by the mind. Let a man, healthy in body and full of strength, hear you say to him: "You do not look well; are you ill?" and let him hear it repeated several times in the course of his conversation with you, and you will find that this healthy individual will soon actually begin to feel quite ill; he will actually feel that something is wrong within him, that his vitality is somewhat low, that his organs are not functioning properly. Fundamentally it makes no difference whether such suggestions come from without or from within, whether they are given by others or given by oneself; the result is the same. Again, it matters not whether the suggestions are made with reference to health, or to age or to death. The body receives these suggestions and harmonizes its condition to these suggestions. There is no doubt that we ourselves weaken our bodies and shorten our lives through our erroneous convictions as to old age and through our thoughts of death.

Also, if you wish to live long, do not lose interest in life. Do not say to yourself, at a certain age: "This world is for young people, I have already passed the stage of youth and ambition, there is nothing left for me but to retire." When one takes this attitude, and segregates himself from the activities of life, he actually passes a death sentence upon himself. By losing interest in life, he undoubtedly hastens his end. In fact, without this interest, life at any time dwindles into a mere process of vegetation and it becomes simply a period of waiting, of waiting for the end. Man must keep on growing, else he withers away. Life does not tolerate stagnation, it does not excuse inaction, it demands that man, who is gifted with powers for action, utilize his powers in creative spheres. A great part of this world is indeed for young people, but an even greater part of this world is for those who have passed the period of youth. Youth occupies the realm of dreams, of exultation, of passion, of fancy;

maturity has for its possession the world of reality, of reason, of achievement. This civilization of ours is not the product of young minds, it is the creation of maturity. The world keeps its most vital place for men of experience and maturity. It matters not, therefore, what your age be, it matters not what your fortune, devote yourself to something useful, identify yourself with something helpful, stand for something vital and effective in human life, and you will reap your reward right here on earth. You will be rewarded by a longer and a happier life. A man of maturity, who has sufficiently provided for his sustenance, can do nothing better than identify himself completely with a spiritual cause, give it his time and his energy, work for its advancement and its growth. There is a tremendous store of life in an ideal, there is eternal youth in a spiritual cause, and the more you identify yourself with it, the more does it lavish upon you of its life, the more does it impart to you of its own vigour and power and youth. An ideal keeps your soul from decrepitude, it keeps your mind from decay, it keeps your body from the weaknesses of old age.

Finally, to prolong your span of life, keep your mind always in a happy state. Never let your spirits droop. Let not external circumstances affect your spirit; let not the inclemency of the weather influence your mood, let not the contact with human society interfere with your natural inner happiness. Do not permit the wealth, the fortune of others, which you may not possess, to throw you into a turmoil of envy or discontent; let not the honors showered upon others bring bitterness to you; let not the luxuries, the splendors, that others display, dim the joys of your own world, of your own possessions, of your own sources of happiness. Do not, moreover, permit your business to be a source of worry and misery to you. Your business will benefit by a happy mental state on your part. If things are well, be glad of your gain; if they are not as you would wish, consider how to make them so, but do not brood over them. For with a happy mind, the difference between struggle and wealth is not so great, and joy can be found with little as well as with much. In order to live long, train yourself for longevity; train yourself for longevity not only at the ebb of

your days, but in your very youth.   Always
let your mind be buoyant, let it be cheerful, let
it be optimistic and hopeful, and you will thereby be depositing treasures of strength for your
advanced days.

God did not designate the number of man's
days on earth.   It was not his design that man
should live three score and ten and no more.
Had it been His law, there would be no exception possible to this pre-ordained span of
existence, for God's laws are uniform and apply
in the same manner to each individual.   The
fact that men die at different ages shows clearly that it was not God's plan to interfere with
man's life, but to let man himself determine
the length of his days.   There is a definiteness
in the period making for birth, for birth or
creation is God's work, but there is no definiteness in death, for man himself, consciously or unconsciously, determines the length of
his life.   God implanted in man a love of life,
a desire for long years, not in order to deceive
him, but because long years were meant for
man to possess and for man himself to attain.
Live therefore always with optimism and cheer;
count not your birthdays and sigh not over

the days that have passed. Think and affirm youth. Withdraw not your interest from life; do not, through indifference, silence your faculties of thought and understanding and enthusiasm. Participate in life, dedicate your efforts particularly to the higher ideals of life; think in terms of life and not of dissolution; and your days will be many on this earth.

THE DIVINE LAW OF ORDER

When our mind steps out for a moment from its mundane interests and begins to reflect upon the encompassing world, it becomes deeply, and even overwhelmingly, impressed by the perfect order which reigns in the whole vast universe. Each star is given its orbit and deviates not from its course. The sun rises and sets with utmost faithfulness and regularity. The seasons succeed each other with perfect timeliness and order. The landscape, the horizon, the rainbow, all are compositions of perfect order. There is order even in the diversified forest, in the variegated field, and in the network of brooks and streams. The law of order governs the very growth of each plant, the very development of each tree, the very formation of each being.

Man, too, was created in strict accord with the law of order. There is order in the formation of his limbs and organs and functions. There is order in his senses and in the action of his vital processes. His heart beats with de-

31

finite rhythm; his eye, his ear receive ethereal vibrations with ordered measure, scale and pitch. Man's tastes love order. His love for beauty is fundamentally a love for order; symmetry, harmony, unity are only phases of aesthetic arrangements in order. Man's primitive conscious development points to a deep desire for order. His early designation of East, West, North and South; his combining of days into weeks and months into years; his invention of numbers, so that he might arrange things in a series, all these are decisive testimony to man's early and instinctive striving for the attainment of order. It is clear, therefore, that man's life was meant to be conducted in accordance with the law of order.

This law holds dominion both over space and over time. Over matters extended in space it shows itself in the form of system; things in nature are arranged in accordance with a systematic design; the very purpose of evolution is to bring more and more system and thereby more perfection into existence. Over things passing through the duration of time, the law of order displays its rule in the form of regularity. In nature, there is stringent, unyielding regularity; the day and the night follow each other in undeviating succession; the motions and position of the heavenly bodies are easily calculable and, without difficulty, predicted far in advance, because of the absolute regularity of their speed; the soil yields its fruit in the accustomed season with the same faithful regularity, and the sea rises and ebbs with predictable punctuality. System and regularity are then the two aspects of the Law of Order. Man's unconscious life, that part of his being which works without his direct control, is also controlled by the divine law of order, and this accounts for the system and regularity that governs all his inner organs and functions. Man's conscious life, that aspect of his being which is directly under the control of his will, should likewise be conducted with system and regularity, in order to attain its utmost of perfection, but here it is where man himself, man's will, must bring the Law of Order to function over his life.

Man must, first of all, keep his mind in order, even as he keeps his house in order. He endeavors to keep his house in order, so that his own aesthetic taste and that of others be satisfied. He must keep his mind in order so that he may see a clearer world (for the mind is the instrument by which the world is perceived), so that his creative faculties may find an easier, smoother pathway for their expression, so that his entire reservoir of mental energy may function with greater economy and yet with greater effectiveness. As a rule, thought springs in the human mind with indiscriminate abundance. The mind thinks many thoughts, but not all thoughts are vital, not all are essential, not all are relevant and useful. There are many thoughts which should be expressed and many others suppressed; there are many thoughts which should be translated into action, and many others which should be banished; many should be cherished and fostered and encouraged, and many others should be incarcerated and starved. Again, many thoughts are merely fanciful, originating only in reverie and fantasy, having no possible connection with life and action, while others are practical, the fruit of experience and springing from common sense. Then, there are thoughts which are unrighteous, impure and vitiating, while there are others of integrity, of

purity, of moral and spiritual elevation. To
bring order, therefore, in the realm of the mind,
means, first of all, to be selective in your
thought, it means to bring the weight of the
mind to bear on that which is useful and beneficial. Do not permit your mental energy to
waste itself on irrelevancies and frivolities; do
not permit your mind to travel in the by-paths
instead of on the highway of life; do not make
small things the outstanding things in your life;
but always utilize the stream of your mind-
energy for the realization of something that
will count in your life and in the life of others.
In order to force the mind to avoid ex-
traneous, insignificant outlets, in order to prevent its wastage, center the mind most vigor-
ously upon the essential object of your thought.
Do not let that object slip from the field of
your mental vision. See it, repeat it, hold it,
and the various currents of your thought,
springing from the different centers of the
mind, will flow in the direction of your vital
goal. There will then be an orderly array of
thought to weigh it and balance it and add
power and depth and meaning to it, and urge
action upon you and bring about its realization.

And just as there must be order in the realm of the mind, so must there also be order in the realm of the heart, that is, in the world of desire. The human heart is a veritable ocean of desires, many of which are good and wholesome, and others of which are quite the contrary; many human desires strive to lead man onward and upward, to refine him and elevate him, others are mere survivals of savage generations. Man is not yet what his better judgment tells him he should be. There are still great distances between himself and the perfect man. Man has indeed risen and made progress, but the distance he has travelled is only a small part of the road that lies before him. The hindrances which chiefly retard his journey to perfection are the unwholesome desires in his disposition. For there are negative as well as positive desires in each one's make-up. There are desires which make for debasement, for destruction; desires which make for envy, jealousy, bitterness, violence, deception. To bring order into his heart, man must select and encourage the wholesome and starve the unwholesome desires within his being. He must identify himself with that which is salutary within him, he must put forth his whole strength in its support. The heart is set in order when conflict between the higher and the lower is removed, when struggling emotions cease their war, when man's desire craves only for the good and the noble.

As order must reign in man's mental and emotional centers so must it also govern the realm of man's conduct and action. There must be system in whatever man does or undertakes. The world is full of interests, it holds out appeals to many aspects of our being, but the world is larger than ourselves, it is impossible for us to encompass all its activities, we cannot identify ourselves with everything that the world offers. We must be selective. We must chose certain aspects of life and make them our own, but no more. We need not do everything, we need not be everywhere, we need not take in every experience or every pleasure, we need not inject our personality into everything, everywhere. Our experiences must not exceed our powers, our individual world must be limited to the proportions of our capabilities. Only then can our life be deep and pleasant and serene.

In following the law of order, not only must
we not seek to take in everything into our
grasp, but even that which measures up to our
powers must be taken in its due course, one
thing at a time. Attend to one thing, and do
the one thing well, and it will be yours; then
you may attend to another thing, then to a
third, and to a fourth; but do not attend to
all at one time, with the same mind. You are
not built to do things in that way, and you
will not do them well. Energy is best utilized
when it is concentrated, when all of it is given
in one direction at any one particular time;
when it is sent into too numerous channels, it is
at once diffused and wasted.

Some minds are trained from early childhood to follow the law of order, but many
minds are not. If you would train yourself
now, remember that the useful thing must always have the claim of priority. The useful
thing *must* be attended to first. The useful
thing is not always the most pleasurable thing;
in fact, it is often the most difficult thing, but it
must be done. And the sooner it is done, the
sooner it is achieved, the easier does the
achievement itself become and the sooner are

its benefits received. If you must postpone, postpone the small things, the trivial things, even the pleasurable things, if necessary, but never the useful things. They must be done. And if you do not do them, some one else will, and you will miss the joy of achievement.

System and regularity are two most vital factors in man's life. They are more essential than power, for power without system is frittered away and never becomes effective; they are more potent than skill, for skill too may be squandered in the absence of system and regularity. Even wisdom, without these two adjutants may become futile; for wisdom, without system and without regularity, may illumine like sudden flashes in the night, but it will fail' to guide one's steps steadily. Let there be system in your thought, selective direction in your desires, regularity in your habits, and you will find your life harmonious with the Divine Law of Order.

THE INFERIORITY COMPLEX

We have heard much during the last several years of a so-called inferiority complex. Psychologists, indeed, have terrified a large number among us with the discovery that an inferiority complex exists in the minds of many. And many, rightly or wrongly, now look upon themselves as the victims of this strange weakness. It is a peculiar fact that man is more prone to magnify his possible debilities than to place a true estimate upon his natural strength. The consciousness of strength will always generate more strength, while the consciousness of and dilation upon a weakness will nurture it and make it stay.

Now what is this inferiority complex? In its simplest terms, it is the consciousness of a handicap in our make-up. This handicap may be physical or mental or even purely imaginary. One who possesses a physical deformity or deficiency, let us say, may become over-conscious of his blemish and look upon himself as an inferior being. This consciousness

of inferiority may grow upon him, it may over-
master him, it may limit him and make him
think that he belongs to an inferior category.
In this way, he loses his self-esteem and dares
not appear or venture where others make their
way and find their happiness.   Or, the individual may be possessed of a mental handicap;
of a poor memory, or a slowness of understanding, or of imperfect powers of observation. The
over-consciousness of his deficiency may greatly interfere with his career and with his happiness. Bear in mind that I do not say that the
defect itself would interfere with his career or
hinder him from happiness, but that the consciousness of it, the worry over it, the strong
attempt to conceal it, would in many ways
block his progress and attainment in life. This
handicap, I have said, may be physical or
mental, or again it may be purely imaginary.
That is to say, the individual does not at all
possess the deficiency of which he imagines
himself to be possessed, but this morbid imagin-
ing nevertheless creates in him a feeling of inferiority which causes him to retire from higher
groups, from higher aims and ambitions, and
close himself up within the narrow closet of

his mind. He imagines himself inferior, and therefore attributes every mishap, every difficulty, every failure to this imagined inferiority.

Let me say that a defect in one's make-up cannot possibly of itself be a cause of failure in life. Our senses, our organs, are only instruments of the mind. We nourish ourselves not so much for the subsistence of our flesh as for the existence and growth of our mind. Our flesh is of no particular value to us; as long as the essence of the human mind is not impaired, blemishes in the body, deficiencies even in the observation processes, cannot prevent man's progress and advancement. The mind can always make its own tools, it can find its own way, it can utilize that which it has in such a fashion as to make up for that which it is denied. We are told that Demosthenes, the greatest orator which the world ever has had, was of a shy disposition, that his organs of speech were defective, that his first appearance as a speaker evoked only ridicule. But his vocal defects, his timidity of disposition, were no drawbacks to his intellect and will. He applied himself assiduously, wholeheartedly to the task of making of himself an orator, and succeeded to the extent that to-day, after the passage of twenty-three centuries, he is still reverenced as the greatest master of all time, in his chosen art. History describes Napoleon as unusually slight and small of stature, and frequently slighted therefor. But he determined in his mind to surpass his physical frailty. He said to himself: "They shall see me big; they shall see me strong; they shall have respect for my height." And they did. There is the splendid American woman, Helen Keller, who, as you know, is deprived of most of her physical senses, and locked in a dark, helpless body. But what is this defective body to the fiery spirit within. The mind within learned to disregard its defective physical organs, it broke down the barriers that obstructed its communion with the world. She, this wonderful woman, refused to be a prisoner all her life. And assuredly she is free.

Therefore we say that a defect or blemish in one's make-up is no cause for failure. Failure begins only when the individual begins to dilate upon his deficiency, brood over it, keep it constantly before him, lament his destiny and always see himself inferior to the rest of his kind.

While this inferiority complex, according to psychologists, manifests itself chiefly where there is an organic defect, there exists quite often another form of inferiority complex which manifests itself in perfectly healthy and sound individuals. There are men and women who would like to know things, would like to do things, would like to create and achieve, and yet make no effort toward such a goal. They look upon themselves as incapable of the big things that others are accomplishing. When difficulties present themselves, when obstacles arise, they do not exert themselves to overcome them, but withdraw from the attempt in the belief that they are of inferior stuff. But they are not inferior either in talent or in power. What they need is self-assertion and a stronger consciousness of duty—the duty which they owe to themselves of giving expression to their faculties and powers, and still more, the duty which they owe to the world of letting it benefit by what they are able to produce and accomplish. Just as the world is indebted to the individual, so is the individual indebted to the world. Just as the world owes the individual opportunity, so does the individual owe the world the effort that utilizes the opportunity. And just as the world offers the individual its treasures of wisdom and enlightenment, so must the individual contribute of his own inspiration, of his own talents to add to the treasures of the world. A consciousness of this fundamental duty will do much to demolish the inferiority complex of many who are not aware of the wealth of capability that resides within them, and therefore make no effort to utilize it.

Those who are fostering within themselves a sense of inferiority, be the cause what it may be, are limiting themselves to a low level. They are drawing, in their minds, a line of demarcation between themselves and what they consider a higher class of mankind. They place themselves among the lower ranks and dare not venture to step out from this self-circumscribed circle. Such an attitude may savor of modesty, but it is not modesty, it is only a handicap and a hindrance to individual progress and happiness. There is no real division between group and group, and between man and man. When a man acts his highest, he belongs among the highest; when he acts his noblest, he belongs to the noble, and only when his acts are low does he belong among the low. This is the true basis of division between the high and the low among mankind. Any other division of humanity is arbitrary and worthless. A man should therefore never consider himself among the inferior; such a view will only interfere with his rise, with his gain, with his development. On the other hand, one should, keeping always to the highest in thought and in act, cherish deep respect for himself. The world respects the man who respects himself. In fact, the respect one receives from the world is commensurate only to the respect one has for himself. The one who is regarded by the world as low has never had a high opinion of himself, and the one esteemed as high, never considered himself among the low. Let us remember that neither wealth nor power are the measures of true rank; those who are only rich are not necessarily among the high, those who are only possessed of power are not necessarily among the high; but the noble *are* among the high, the good *are* among the high, the men who express their faculties and abilities in achievement *are* among the high, and this high station is open to all.

An inferiority complex, we see, may develop and take on any shape or form, and may find its source in numberless causes. In no instance, however, is there a true cause for inferiority. Inferiority does not exist outside of its existence in a human mind. God created man with courage, with strength, with power, and when these divine gifts are utilized, man cannot but find himself among the highest of his kind.

HOW TO FACE SUFFERING

Why does man suffer? This question has been asked by men of all generations. If everything that exists in this world is here for a purpose, to what end is human suffering? If God is good, if He desires the well-being of those He created,—for that is what goodness implies—why is there suffering among His children?

Various minds have offered different answers to this perplexing question. Some have put forth the belief that suffering is a retributive measure, that it is a punishment for sin committed in this world. Others have maintained that suffering is a purifying, preparatory process. Man suffers in this world in order to receive blessing and bliss in the world to come; man is cleansed here, that he might take his place among the pure and righteous of mankind in heaven. Another view-point on suffering is to be found in the teachings of the Mohammedan faith, and is also expressed by some of the philosophers of the past century, and that is that suffering is the destiny of the world and of man, that misery is inherent in existence.

In Jewish Science, we subscribe to none of these theories. We regard them, on the contrary, as erroneous and misleading. We do not believe that suffering is a punishment for sin; we do not believe that God follows the doings of each man in order to record them and mete out punishment for misdoings, in the fashion of a human tribunal. This is entirely too primitive a conception of God's ways and methods. Man may punish *himself* by selecting and following that which is hurtful to his being, but in such a case it is he who is inflicting injury upon himself, no power from without is involved. Nor do we believe, in Jewish Science, that suffering is a purifying factor, for do we not see innocent and righteous men suffering, though there may be nought in their lives that has need of cleansing and purifying? Moreover, does suffering always have a purifying effect? Are we not witness to the fact that suffering is often the cause of deeper doubt and even of desperate conduct, contrary to the ways of God? Nor do we hold to the philosophy which

looks upon suffering as the law of existence. On
the contrary, we see the world in the very
opposite light; we know that God, in His goodness, did not destine man to suffer, that, on the
other hand, it was the Divine intention that
man find joy and be happy all the days of his
life; it is to this very end, we believe, that He
filled the world with sunshine, with abundance,
with plenty, with beauty and with harmony;
it is to this very purpose that He lavished upon
man faculties, and aspirations, and hopes, all
this that he may find greater and deeper fields
for happiness. No! God's design was to make
joy, not misery, the goal of existence. How
then is it that there *is* so much suffering in this
world? To answer this troublous question, we
shall endeavor first to understand the nature
of suffering and then learn how to face and
eliminate it.

Suffering has its source either in physical
pain or in mental distress, and all forms of
suffering may be placed under the one or the
other head, sometimes under both. As to
physical pain, let me say that God created it
in order to guard and preserve man. This may
sound paradoxical, and yet it is true. I say

that God called physical pain into existence in order to shield and sustain man. Pain is not an end in itself, it is a means to an end. The object of pain is not to make man suffer, but to warn man of some irregularity in his conduct, of some excess in his habits, of some disharmony among the various organs and processes of his body, of some violation, conscious or unconscious, of the divine laws set in his being.

The child that touches fire suffers intense pain. Yet this pain is not intended as a punishment, but as a warning; it urges the child to withdraw its little hand from the flame. If there were no pain the child would continue playing with the fire until its little hand were made helpless and useless, since it is in the nature of fire to burn and destroy. Pain at the first touch of the flame serves as a protector and a preserver. Pain, in this instance, is also a kind teacher; it will not only make the child withdraw its hand from the flame at the first instant, but it will prevent the child's touching it again. The painful experience will create an inhibition in the child, which will counteract any desire to play again with the red flame.

An individual who experiences pain in his digestive organs, will, through this pain, be aroused to the fact that he has taken into his system something harmful to him; this pain will set him to discover the cause and correct immediately his condition. Without this warning of pain, the poisonous substance would continue to be taken in, would be assimilated more and more deeply into his system, and gradually devour the very vitals of his being,— all this without his being at all conscious of his true condition. Without pain man would be unable to realize the invasion of danger, and would expose himself unknowingly to corroding ailments, that would shorten his days and in time destroy him. The realization which pain brings with it, enables him to arrest the progress of the unhealthy condition that the pain indicates. Pain is therefore not an enemy, but a helper, a preserver of man. Pain stands at the threshold of consciousness, examines every incoming sensation, tests the nature of every substance brought into the system, is carefully alert of our habits and manner of living, and, if it detects poison in our food, excess in our habits, irregularity and disorder in our method of living, immediately raises its red signal of danger by pricking us, jarring us, causing us pressure and discomfort. And the pain does not cease until we have delved into the cause of our difficulty and proceeded to remove it.

I have said that suffering may consist of mental distress as well as of physical pain, and that physical pain is indeed a divine device to call attention to some disharmony in our being. But to what end is mental affliction? Let me say that no end is served through mental suffering. It does not serve as a warning of harm, but it is harmful in itself. While physical pain is a divine provision to safeguard the individual, mental distress is not at all the creation of God; it is the creation of man himself. But who is the man that desires to create suffering unto himself? No man, of course, would consciously afflict himself, but unconsciously, unknowingly, he does. How does mental distress arise? Mental distress has its origin in a pessimistic interpretation of life and of the world in general. Mental distress arises through worry and fear. When men see danger everywhere, failure at every step, privation and degradation in the future, they become a

prey to worry and fear, and in consequence
their mind sinks into deeper and deeper suffering.   There, as you will observe, are three distinct steps leading to mental suffering.   First,
there is the act of seeing life and interpreting
the future in pessimistic terms, then a state of
worry and fear over a future or over a state of
affairs so perceived; and finally, through this
worry and fear, the falling into a state of
misery and mental affliction. You can see
thereby that mental affliction is the creation of
man himself. It is his erroneous outlook upon
life that brings him worry and then distress.
He is himself responsible for his mental agony,
for he can just as well interpret life and read
his future in optimistic terms. Instead of facing the approaching future with despondency,
let him face it with hope, and he will escape
the clutches of worry, and be moreover more
true in his judgment. Instead of saying to
himself, "I see dark days before me," let him
say and think, "I see that brighter days will
come, must come." Instead of thinking of
what he has lost, let him think of what he has;
instead of thinking of what he cannot have,
let him think of what it is in his power to

have; there will be a sudden lightening of his mental load, he will become a different being.

Let a man never allow his hope to droop or desert him, and he need never suffer mental anguish. With hope a man can face every situation, every difficulty, every calamity, even the severest pain, and emerge without anguish of spirit. I say even the severest pain, for the greatest pain known to mankind is the pain of childbirth, and yet the hope that a child is coming into existence makes even this pain easy and immediately forgotten; and as far as we know, there is no woman who is not willing to take this pain in order that her hope be realized. With hope, obstacles are removed, barriers are destroyed, all counterpressure is obliterated.

And how is hope acquired, when things are dim and apparently without hope? Hope is acquired and sustained through faith—faith in an invisible Power that sustains and helps, faith in a benevolent Father who preserves and shelters and provides, faith in God who watches tenderly over the destiny of all whom He created. Have faith that He will watch over you today as He did yesterday, in the future as He did in the past, and your hope will not fade, whether in this circumstance or in another circumstance.

Remember that suffering is of two types and that each must be faced and met in a different fashion. Physical suffering, pain, must be viewed as a warning; take it soon, and it will save you from greater suffering. Do not seek only to alleviate the pain, but endeavor to change your habits, your methods of living, your food, in order to eliminate the causes of which pain is the warning signal. As to mental suffering, change your outlook upon life and upon things. Strengthen your faith in God, and thereby your hope, and you will know of no mental distress.

FROM POSTPONEMENT TO FAILURE

There is often a marked division between the human judgment and the human will. There are instances where the will is stronger than discretion; where it refuses to be guided or controlled by prudence, where it casts off the reins of thought and breaks violently away from the anchor of reason; it then becomes the perpetrator of the most extravagant acts. That is what we mean by impulsive, impetuous action, when the will tears itself away from the influence and restraint of logic, and goes on a rampage. It acts then in a manner that it usually later regrets. On the other hand, there are more instances where the will is weaker than judgment; where reason plans, and understanding decides, and discretion urges, but the will is unwilling, it is too indolent to actualize the decisions of thought. The mind is bent in the right direction, it plans correctly, it dreams of great achievements and conquests and reformations, but the dreams remain only dreams, the will refuses to translate them into action.

It does not antagonize them, but it postpones them. "Yes," it says, "I'll do it—later, to-morrow, some other time, but not today." And in this postponement lies the secret of so many failures, of so much mediocrity.

The sage has said, "That which is essential to life should not be delayed." There are definite things in life which man must not only not procrastinate, but, if necessary, force himself to do. The things which man should not postpone, are, essentially, three: he should not delay an act of achievement, he should not delay an act of kindness, he should not delay his search for God.

When we say that he should not delay an act of achievement, we do not mean that he should rush to the other extreme, work each day with exhausting intensity and overwhelming haste, overstrain his energies and overtax his powers in order to accomplish all his intended tasks without delay. We mean particularly that it is dangerous to delay the beginning of an essential task. Begin to achieve today; then follow it up regularly, faithfully and serenely every day. There are two ways of meeting life; one is by doing things, by doing them steadily every day; the other is by postponing them from day to day, from week to week, from year to year. By *doing* every day, man moves forward; he becomes master of his task, expert in his calling, leader in his sphere of activity; each day finds him more self-reliant, richer in experience and in progress, richer in knowledge and in understanding, richer in vision and in maturity. But he who is constantly postponing, who is always dreaming but never doing, who is always planning to begin tomorrow but not today, is foredoomed to failure in life. For while he may see, with his imagination, many conquests of which he is the hero, while he may dream of brave deeds and gigantic accomplishments, in reality he moves not from his place; he gains neither in experience nor in wisdom; he neither grows nor attains.

The man who *does*, and does not delay, finds himself daily growing nearer to his natural dimensions. By this I mean that each man is much greater, much keener, much more resourceful than he first considers himself to be; each faculty, each power in him is possessed of deep reservoirs of energy, of layers of sagacity and acumen, of keenness and creativeness. When man achieves regularly, his hidden powers come to the fore; his personality assumes larger proportions, his individuality gains in dimension; each year finds him bigger than the preceding year. On the other hand, with one who postpones, the personality shrinks; faculties become dormant, gifts become atrophied and powers starved from lack of expression. There is a stunting and impoverishing of the whole being.

Then, he who has formed the habit of unprocrastinated action, becomes independent. He who thinks for himself need not rely upon the thoughts of others; he who acts for himself need not depend upon the acts of others; he who can achieve and sustain himself need not depend upon the achievement and support of others. Through his diligence, he finds the way, discovers the method, and attains the goal by himself. The other, who delays, is always a dependent being; he is always helpless and seeking upon whom to rely. He refuses to think for himself, hence he is dependent upon the thought of others; he refuses to guide himself, and must therefore be guided by the counsel of others; he does not act for himself, hence he is dependent upon the acts of others; he does not attain, he does not achieve by himself, hence he is dependent on the achievement of others. He cannot point to anything which is the creation of his own efforts, the product of his own power. Postponement has killed his birthright of achievement. The sage therefore insists that "that which is essential to life should not be postponed." Achievement is fundamental and vital to life; it is a part of life's program, it is the purpose for which faculties and powers have been given, it is the requirement of civilization.

And just as it is ruinous to delay an act of achievement, so is it also to postpone the expression of kindness. There is more tenderness in man than he usually manifests, there is more goodness, more charity, more generosity in him than he generally displays. Man shows extraordinary tardiness and backwardness in expressing his benevolent emotions. Somehow, he prefers to keep his tender self in the background, veiled from sight, refusing it its required freedom of action. It is for this reason that so much bitterness, so much discord, so much misunderstanding exists among men; for when the sympathetic self occupies only an insignificant seat in the back of human consciousness, the relationship among men becomes rigid, cold, formal and indifferent. What does mankind need today more than all else? Mankind needs more charity, more love, more sympathy, more generosity. It needs the full expression of the tender human emotions.

An expression of the tender emotions is, in religious terms, nothing other than obedience to the voice of God. For how does God speak to man? Does he communicate with him in terms of language? No. This was the primitive conception of God's speech with man. God speaks to man through man's own vision and man's own emotions. In his vision, God shows man the right way, He points out to him the correct goal; through his emotions, God urges man to *do* good. Each sympathetic emotion that arises in the human breast, each benevolent feeling which flutters through the field of his consciousness, are words of God spoken to man. In this sense, to carry out a benevolent impulse is to follow the behest of God.

The augmentation of sympathy and charity

among mankind depends upon the charity and sympathy which each individual expresses. There can be no kindness in the multitude if there is none in the individual, for the multitude is only an aggregation of individuals. There can therefore be no charity in mankind if there is none in man. There can be no goodness, no generosity in the human world, if there is none in the act of each man. Here is where every individual counts; here every heart occupies a place of station and prominence; here everyone can and must contribute to the advancement of humanity. Therefore, it is a sin to postpone the expression of a kindly or generous impulse. The more one delays an act of nobility or a deed of kindness, the fainter grows the desire for its performance. The more one refuses to listen to the voice of God, the more restrained does the divine voice become. Shun therefore this fatal delay. Do not whisper to yourself: "I'll do it tomorrow, I'll do it by-and-by, I'll see first what others are doing." Let me say to you that when an opportunity arises to do good, consider it a privilege to do it, whether that be to help a stricken neighbor, or to advance a helpful cause, or to promote the welfare of humanity at large. Here is an occasion, and the only occasion, where you must make haste, for if you do not, that kindly feeling, that generous impulse will leave you. Your heart will remain cold and frozen, to your own detriment. Why always follow the example of others, let others follow your example; when you do good, you do right, and when you are in the right, you can afford to stand in advance of the rank of mankind and lead others.

One must not delay an act of achievement, one must not delay the expression of a tender emotion, and, finally, one must not delay the search for God. Men today are too apt to postpone this quest, to defer their religious life to their later days. When a man is strong and ambitious, especially when he is successful, he often thinks that he has little need of religion. We find among our people more apathy than atheism, more indifference and postponement than conscientious skepticism. But a man needs God at every stage and in every station of his life. God is not only a Sustainer and a Helper but He is the very Fountain of life, the very Essence of existence. Whence this beautiful light, this radiant sunshine? From God. Whence the eternal planets, the eternal stars? From God. Whence our earth with its abundance and plenty? Whence the beauteous fields, the luxuriant forests, the overwhelming mountains, the refreshing streams? Whence the multitudinous forms of life? Whence man? From God. All, all from God. God is the all-embracing Power, the all-sustaining and all-containing Presence. Without the consciousness of God, man, though firmly established in his own sphere, finds himself a mere transient wanderer in this world. Without God man can have no philosophy of life; without God he can have no ideal of life; without God he can have no conception of the future of his own life; without God he cannot embrace in the circumference of his life, the life of the world, nor does he feel any union between his own life and the life of the world; without God, man's life becomes very small, his world outlook without significance; life becomes a series of small pleasures, a chain of trifles and trivialities, a process merely of satisfying the senses, of gratifying the appetites. No! Man can afford neither to stray from God, nor defer the experience of a religious life to his later days. A delay in religious expression is a loss —a loss in idealism, a loss in spirituality; and the more the religious consciousness is deferred, the weaker, the more famished does it become, and man's life loses its finest aspect thereby.

Man, for his own highest good, must tear himself away from the slothful habit of postponement, for postponement leads only to failure. Man is born with creative powers which he must express for himself and for the world; he is born to achieve; therefore he must not delay an act of achievement. Through the expression of kindness, man comes closer to the heart of his fellowman; only through the spread of the tender emotions will brotherhood and happiness be generated in this world; therefore man must never delay an act of kindness. Finally, man's elevation, his vision, his help and his strength, his guidance and his support are attained only through God; therefore let him not delay this highest expression of all—his search for God.

SELF-CONFIDENCE

We find that there is a marked contrast between what man is and what he thinks himself to be. We find, as a rule, that man is more prone to underestimate than to overestimate himself. This he does not so much because of modesty, but rather through ignorance of his true capabilities. There are powers and capacities and creative energies hidden in the depths of man's consciousness of which he has no knowledge at all. Man knows more of the world outside himself than of the world within himself; he has a clearer conception and a truer evaluation of that which is about him than of that which is within him. That which is about him he can discern readily through his senses, that which is within is beyond the grasp of the senses. It must be discovered by an entirely different method. If it were possible to make all human capacities visible and project them into the exterior world, they would occupy immeasurable space, they would extend to enormous heights, they would manifest a dazzling variety of brightness and a multiplicity of color. For this is what man's capacities actually achieve whenever they *are* given full expression. They build gigantic structures, they enter into vast enterprises, they exercise themselves in tremendous achievements, each of which is only a manifestation, only an extension of man's inborn capability.

How then is a man to discover his inner powers? Not through contemplation, but through action. Human capacity is like a spring of water concealed under the surface of the ground. You must dig and make an outlet for it and then it will yield its refreshing stream in greater and greater abundance. One must make the attempt to achieve, one must make the effort, must act, and then the inner capacities will unfailingly assert themselves. Plans will formulate themselves in the mind, visions to be realized will make their appearance on the horizon of the imagination, fertile thoughts, wholesome thoughts, will flock in from all the corners of the mind, and the individual will find himself growing and gaining, he will find his powers unfolding themselves, reaching out and achieving higher and still higher things.   If you would know what powers you possess, engage whole-heartedly upon a task, a serious task, and all that is within you will come forward to aid in its consummation.

There are two ways of engaging upon a task. One is to approach it listlessly, or with indifference; the other is to attack it with optimism and with confidence in oneself.   Let one go to his task half-heartedly, hesitatingly, with a consciousness of possible failure; with such a state of mind, he cannot go very far.   Without trust in his ability, without confidence in himself, he is prone to be faced with a series of disappointments.   Every difficulty will discourage him, every obstacle will send him into retreat, every hardship, every barrier, will dishearten him and cast him down.   Without confidence in himself, he may dream beautiful dreams, he may see visions of achievement, but his dreams will leave no trace of reality behind them.   Without confidence in himself, man's true abilities remain inactive.   When a man tells himself that he cannot do it, then it matters not how easy the task may be, he will not do it.   For thoughts come only in proportion to the desire with which they are invoked, faculties act in accordance with the invitation which is extended to them. If that be coldly offered, there is a cold reticence on their part, and they will assert themselves reluctantly, if at all. The individual will then complain of the circumstances in which he is placed, he will find fault with his destiny, he will blame his star, when all that he lacks is simply belief in himself.

On the other hand, let him go to his task with trust in his powers, with confidence in himself, and he will find himself working whole-heartedly and enthusiastically, with courage and with zeal, bent on high achievement. The man with confidence in himself always aims high, and these heights are not mere fancies for his imagination to toy with and enjoy, but they are goals to be striven for and attained. The man with confidence in himself does not stop at difficulties. Nothing can discourage him, nothing can stand between him and his goal. A man with confidence in himself is never down, or if he is down, he is down only to gather new forces, to make new plans, to make new combinations, to find new ways that will enable him to rise to even greater heights. A man with confidence in himself never murmurs against unfavorable circumstances, for he is master of his environment, he can mould and fashion and determine the circumstances of his life. He does not complain of lack of opportunities, he makes his opportunities; he is not at all anxious to walk on trodden paths, he paves his own road, he makes his own world.

Self-confidence is not egotism, it is not conceit. The conceited boasts of what he can do, the man of self-confidence just does it. The conceited does not believe in himself, but he wishes others to believe in him. The man of self-confidence fundamentally believes in himself, and is not much concerned as to the opinion of others. The conceited is cowardly at heart, his intense desire for the good opinion of others is only the expression of his need to overcome the poor opinion he has of himself. The man of self-confidence is heroic at heart, he realizes his own strength and is independent of the judgment of others. Conceit is a vice, self-confidence is a virtue.

There is magic in self-confidence, there is power in the thought: *I can.* As we read the lives of great men, we find that the thought common to them all was: *I can.* Each one, in his field of achievement, entered into action with the thought: I can. *I can* has been the inscription in the heart of every valiant man, whose deeds of daring have been recorded in history; *I can* has been the watchword of every explorer and inventor; *I can* has been the faith of every pioneer and every builder of civilization; *I can* has been the power behind every one who has thrown himself into the doing of big tasks, who has entered into gigantic enterprises, who has made an overwhelming success of his life. They can build who believe they can, they can achieve who believe they can, they can conquer who believe they can. The world acclaims not the one who thinks great thoughts, but the one who does great things. The world gives credit not to the one who cherishes noble thoughts, but to the one who does noble things. The doer is the one whom the world holds high. And to be a doer one must possess the magic of self-confidence.

Fundamentally, every man has the elements that make for achievement and for greatness, but he must have, or if he have not, must develop, the self-confidence to bring them into action. In developing self-confidence, one must, first of all, avoid atmospheres which discourage, people who dishearten. Men who discourage you are your enemies, men who express only sympathy for you are your enemies, men who are always sorry for you, who always have a pitying nod for you, are your enemies. They may be so unconsciously; they may be seeking only to show you their compassion, they may only be expressing friendship in that manner, but such an expression of friendship does an injury that only an enemy can perpetrate. One who pities you, or bemoans your fate with you, sinks into you the impression that there is something pitiful and miserable about you. He thereby dampens your spirit of action, weakens your daring, kills your enterprise, and helps to keep you down in a state of self-depreciation and self-pity. A true friend will never show you compassion or sympathy, but he will encourage you. Instead of sympathizing with you in your failure, he will minimize your failure; he will express his confidence in your ability and trust in your powers; he knows, and he says it, that you will rise again, in fact, that you *must* rise and achieve and conquer again. Only this, is the attitude of a friend, and none other. Keep far away from sympathy, keep away from those who show you a compassionate countenance; for they kill self-confidence.

Affirm self-confidence. By affirming self-confidence, you are praying for it. One should not hesitate to pray for the effacement of any defect in his being. Man must always do his best, but when his own powers are found to be wanting, he must not hesitate to appeal to the Divine Mind for help. Just as one prays for health, for hope, for cheer, so should he also pray for self-confidence; for the lack of self-confidence is a weakness, it is a deficiency in the self-assertive centers, and should be conquered. Affirm earnestly, whole-heartedly: "The God-consciousness in me expresses itself in self-confidence." Your faint-heartedness, your hesitancy, will vanish, and you will hear a voice within you urging you to do, to achieve, to fully express your powers.

THE LAW OF COMPENSATION

There is, without a doubt, a divine law of compensation—a law which brings about the reward of the good and the punishment of the evil. Formerly we were taught that this divine law was operative only in the life hereafter. The just, we were told, were rewarded there with everlasting joy, and the wicked were doomed to eternal suffering. As a corollary to this theory, the human imagination has invented a great variety of suffering for the sinful as well as an infinitude of joys for the good. But the theory of heaven and hell is strictly a human theory. In Jewish Science, we believe indeed in a hereafter, in an existence following this earthly life; we know that while man's form is subject to change, his essence is indestructible, his life is made of eternal substance. But we cannot give credence to theories that have emanated from human fancy and with the object of directing and influencing human conduct through the whip of fear. Let us bear in mind, by the way, that there is no mention in the Sacred Scriptures of heaven and hell as places of reward and punishment, and that this invention is, strictly speaking, a post-Biblical one, originating with the expositors and expounders of religion. Each sage and commentator, we find, gives his own version of the pleasures of heaven and the agonies of the nether world. They are also of diverse opinions as to which of human acts are deserving of eternal reward, and are equally at variance as to which of human evils merit eternal punishment. In general, we find that the more cruelty a sage had witnessed in this world, the more torturous experiences did he inject into pictures of purgatory; the more he experienced need and want in his own life or witness it in the lives around him, the more did he portray heaven as a place of abundance and plenty, a place of endless wealth and fortune.

By declaring that the divine law of compensation becomes effective in the hereafter, theologians have given an easy answer to the eternal question: Why do the wicked so often prosper and the righteous so often suffer? Why do men of dishonesty and duplicity and crookedness sometimes accumulate fortunes,

while men of integrity and righteousness sometimes fail?   The theologians have answered
these questions by asserting that both the
righteous and the evil-doers will receive their de-
serts in the world to come, the good in eternal
joy and the evil in eternal suffering.   In fact,
all theological justice is based on this theory,
that the righteous will inherit eternity, while
the wicked will be cut off from all blessing.

This theory of divine compensation is not at
all in harmony, however, with the one we foster
in Jewish Science.   It is our conviction that
every law laid down by the Divine Mind, carries with it its reward and its punishment, and
that this reward or punishment is not imposed
from without, nor delayed to some future time
or sphere, but constantly accompanies the law
itself.   It is exceedingly essential that we comprehend fully this procedure of reward and
punishment.   The poverty-stricken theologians
who lived in a closely confined garret, pictured
heaven as a place of magnificent spaciousness,
sumptuously equipped, brilliantly illuminated
and beautified.   The poor sage who suffered
cold and hunger saw in heaven a place of abundance, of plenty,—in fact, a vast dining palace

wherein the pious, famished till now, sit around a groaning board and rejoice. We realize, however, that these are but the creations of a longing human fancy, and no more. We see the problem in a different light. Reward, we all understand, is the attainment of happiness, punishment the subjugation to unhappiness. All laws created by the Divine Mind were intended primarily to bring happiness; a compliance with them never fails therefore to bring happiness, while a violation of them never fails to bring misery and unhappiness. There is no special reward for the pious, there is no irrelevant compensation for the just and the righteous; the rewards of justice and integrity and uprightness lie in the acts of justice and integrity and uprightness. God, in His goodness, created laws that make for growth, for progress, for self-preservation, for health, for strength; a compliance with these laws always brings growth, progress, health, long life, happiness; an infringement of these laws hinders progress, breaks down health, and brings wretchedness. We can see that human law is patterned after Divine Law. There are no special rewards offered for compliance with the laws of man, except that which is inherent in those very laws; one who conducts himself properly as a member of the social order or as a citizen of the land, is not given any special compensation, but on the other hand, one who violates the law of the land, is punished. For the law was intended for peace, for harmony, for happiness in the land, and he who complies with it gains in peace, in harmony and in happiness; while he who violates the law is immediately removed from peace, from harmony and from happiness. However, because the human law is arbitrary, the punishment it inflicts upon its infractors is also arbitrary and imposed from without, through a tribunal of justice; but not so with the Divine Law which is fundamental and immutable and therefore carries the punishment for its violation within itself. The human law, finding its origin in human limitation, needs testimony and verification; the Divine law, expressing the Infinite, the Omniscient, needs no verification, and therefore the reward or the punishment is immediate; there is no delay of justice.

The divine law of compensation is effective both in man's conscious and unconscious life.

It is effective, for example, in man's health. When a man falls ill, whether his ailment is organic or functional, whether it shows itself in pain or in depression, there is always behind it, as its cause, a violation, of one kind or another, of the Divine Law. No man falls ill of a sudden, that is, without cause. Even those who have not been conscious of any cause for their illness, may be assured it has followed in compliance with the law of compensation. Man's life was given him to enjoy it, he was placed here on earth to receive its blessings and share abundantly in happiness; if one finds himself wanting in these, and, on the contrary, finds himself in misery, he may be certain that something in his conduct, his manner, his habits, is the cause of his wretchedness. He is only receiving a measure of the law of compensation.

A man may make himself ill through overwork. God implanted in man a definite measure of energy, to be used, but not abused. With his store of energy, a man is capable of working a definite number of hours each day, but no more. If man insists on overworking, on overstraining his energies, on overtaxing his capacities, on neglecting his life for the sake of a living, the law of compensation will check off this abuse against him, and sooner or later his frame will rebel; he will find himself feeble and even helpless before his time. A man must work, he must labor, but he must not overwork. Health is a more valuable treasure than wealth, each man knows that, how then can he afford to spend so much of his health for the little of wealth he may obtain in return. Overwork is a violation of one of the divine laws, and therefore brings its punishment in destroyed health and energy.

And just as one must not overwork himself, so must he not underwork himself, for this too is dangerous. Man's energies must find expression, man's capacities must find an outlet, man's thoughts and feelings must work and create and achieve. If these are doomed to silence and inactivity, if man refuses to express himself, his creative energies shrink, his power of thought loses its vitality, enthusiasm and interest and concentration vanish, and they leave behind them a sensation of uneasiness, emptiness, restlessness and depression. For self-expression through work is a divine law, and its violation brings sure punishment.

Likewise, let a man lose his hold on faith, a power which is vital and natural to man, and his life becomes emptied of purpose and happiness. Man was born to live in faith, to trust God, to pray to God, to seek His help, to invoke His blessing, to appeal to Him for health, and strength, and cheer and hope, to turn to Him in all trials and difficulty. When man lives by faith, when he applies it in every turn of his life, he is obeying a divine law; and his reward is great, for God never fails him, his earnest prayer is never lost, his hopes meet no disappointments, his efforts are crowned with success. When man shakes off faith, he subjects himself to the punishment of worry and forebodings and fear; his mind opens itself to discouragement, to doubt and to disharmony. Any difficulty will dishearten him, any weakness will terrify him, any hardship drive him down. Without faith, the world becomes a place of hazard and peril, life becomes an uncertainty and even a burden.

Righteous conduct, too, is a divine law, and its pursuit is followed by compensation in this very world. The most righteous may not, perhaps, always be the most successful, at least from a worldly point of view; that is, their efforts may not always be compensated with abundance and wealth. But their reward is attained in their own inner state of harmony and happiness. From the viewpoint of the individual, all labor, all enterprise, all achievements, are only channels for the attainment of happiness. Wealth is not desired as an end in itself; for wealth is a soulless bulk, it cannot therefore speak to the soul of man, it cannot fill his heart; man cherishes wealth only for the possible happiness that he may gain through it. Happiness through wealth is only a possibility, often it proves a mirage; but happiness through righteousness is always a surety. The righteous man is always filled with an inner harmony and a keen happiness, even in humble circumstances, which the unrighteous, though in the midst of abundance, can never experience. Righteousness is its own reward and unrighteousness its own punishment; for while the unrighteous may prosper, while he may, at times, gain apparent advantages, yet he fails to secure happiness; there is too much disharmony in his soul, too much rebellion in his conscience, too much violation of the finer emotions, which refuse to be silent and pacified. Unrighteousness may attain to possessions, but it can never attain happiness in this world.

Reward and punishment, we see, do not wait for the hereafter. They are experienced here in this world, they accompany man's every action, just as his shadow, in daylight, accompanies his every step. The right—the right action, the right conduct, the right thought, the right mode of living, the right attitude, the right faith—are always rewarded. The wrong, no matter what that be, is always punished.

WORK AND OVERWORK

One of the great blessings in human life is work. Work gives man his interest in life; it makes life worth living. When a man identifies himself with a task, when he lends it his time, his energy and his effort, his day becomes full, his spirit charged with purposefulness. Work also is a necessary stimulant to the faculties and powers of man, for man's truest development is brought about through work. The mind grows through thinking, the muscles gain in strength through toiling, the will acquires power through acting and creating. Each day of accomplishment, each act of achievement, leaves the faculties keener and deeper, better capable of comprehending and coping with responsibilities and exigencies. Finally, work unites man with humanity, it makes room for man among his kind. Fundamentally, mankind is a corporate organization, the advancement of which depends chiefly upon the efforts of its membership. Every endeavor, every effort, every enterprise, every task to which the individual lends him-

self, though directly it is for his own benefit,
yet indirectly and ultimately it is for the benefit
of the vast organization of mankind. Compensation is given to the toiler, but his toil goes
ultimately to mankind; profit goes to the enter-
priser, but the inherent benefits of the enterprise go to mankind; rewards are lavished upon
the man of talent, but the fruits of his talent
are for the pleasure of mankind. The work
of each individual does therefore ultimately
count for the betterment and advancement of
mankind. Work is, we see, not only a source
of self-gain and self-growth and self-expansion,
but it is also the source from which proceeds
the gain and growth and expansion of mankind.

But while work is a source of strength, overwork is a source of weakness. Man is indeed
possessed of many capabilities, he is gifted
with numerous and deep powers, but he also
has limitations in his nature. Whatever he
does, he must do with moderation, with effort
proportionate to his strength and power. For
if he oversteps the boundary line of his natural
resources, he will do himself an injury. And
just as work is a blessing, so is overwork an
evil. For overwork does not develop the mind,

it destroys it; it does not bring happiness into our life, it banishes it; it does not add to our strength and peace of mind, but, on the contrary, it is the cause of debility and disquietude.

Overwork means simply doing more than we can, and therefore, more than we should. Working long hours, without allowing sufficient time for recreation and rest; crowding into one mind that which should normally be carried by two or more minds; overloading the nervous system with burdens greater than it is capable of carrying with serenity; all this means overwork. Overwork implies the incessant driving of the body to states of fatigue and exhaustion, the exercise of the will at the expense of health and strength and rest and peace. Man is born for work but not for overwork; he is here, indeed, for creation and action, but not for over-exertion and exhaustion. Man is not a mere machine to be wound up and lubricated only for production, man is also a conscious being; his labor must bring him joy, his efforts must yield him delight, his task must not break down the frame of his being.

Here we face the problem which touches so keenly the life of the American people. Through habit, through erroneous standards and desires, through materialistic ideals, the people of this land have created for themselves new rates of speed and new standards of action. Human beings labor here with entirely too much energy and too much haste, with too much recklessness and too much intensity. Observe the business man in action, and you will wonder whence this tremendous energy,— the energy that watches over every one, that observes everything, that worries over everything, that becomes aroused to indignation over every error, that plans aggrandisement, that fights competition, that pours itself out continuously without a let-up. Such a continuous drive on all the powers and faculties, is entirely too strenuous, too exacting, too injurious to the human system.

It is because such a mode of work is very common among us, that the people of this land, more than that of any other land, are subject to the ailment known as neurasthenia, which means simply nervous exhaustion. The human system can indeed stand a great deal of strain, the human mind can carry many burdens, the human body can undertake great labor; but man cannot bear *too much* strain, he cannot carry *too many* burdens, his body cannot resist overwork. When these are continuously forced upon his system, it gives way and feebleness and helplessness are the results. Overwork can make strong men weak, creative men passive, young men prematurely old.

Realizing the effects of overwork upon our system, realizing that this overtaxing of our nervous system only prepares misery for coming days, we must change our habits and our hours of work. We must change our very attitude towards our work. Our work must, first of all, be a pleasure to us, not a burden. There are two fundamental factors either of which will compel us to work. One of these is the necessity for making a living, the second is the need of doing something. And the one is as important as the other. There is a great inner urge to do something. The mind desires some objective upon which it may exercise itself. With every comfort in the world, but without anything to do, life becomes monotonous and depressing and empty of purpose and meaning. On the other hand, work for which the individual has no taste and no desire, is a burden, making the day tiresome and life miserable. In the ideal state, an individual is kept occupied with a task in which he delights; such work does not distress him, nor easily tax him. When an individual enjoys his work, its monetary aspect loses its prime significance; unfavorable circumstances do not easily distress him, adversity does not crush him, his mind, his body do not easily give way. Therefore an individual must make every effort to select or find work which naturally brings him joy.

Then, the individual must train himself to work with poise and with ease. Working strenuously becomes a habit, working with poise is also a habit. Those who labor with ease do not achieve less than those who toil with strain. Observe two individuals with opposite methods of work, the one laboring with intensity and haste, the other, at the same task, with ease and poise. The one who works hurriedly will, as a rule, produce more during the first half of the day, but his energies, during the second half, will ebb very low; there will be a strong tendency to fatigue, the work will lack in accuracy, it will show deficiency in concentration, there will be marked gaps in attention, a weakening of the power of judgment, and a strong tendency to error. This is not the case with the one who is working with ease; there is a smooth evenness in his day, there being little, if any, demarcation between the earlier and the later hours of the day; the mind continues clear-cut, exact, and with its utmost of efficiency. In the end, his work counts for not less, if not for more, than that of the one who has worked with rush and strain; and he is left, moreover, with his body unimpaired, his nerves unfrayed, his reserve of power and strength still untouched.

Finally, one must have definite hours for his work. One must not be identified with his task through every hour of the day. There must be some period in each day when the individual is entirely disengaged from his labors, when his mind is not centered on his business or on his routine, when his energies shift from their day-long course. There must be certain hours in each day for domestic, or recreative or social activities, or merely for repose and ease. During these recreative hours, man's working energies retire and become recharged with strength. His powers of concentration and action relax in order to gain new vitality and freshness. It is only by the alternation of hours of labor with hours of ease that man becomes enabled to work efficiently and to enjoy his work; it is only by observing a rhythm between work and leisure that he is enabled to give the best that is in him, and reach the highest results.

Our work need not be our burden, if we select it aright to meet our capacities; it need not be our oppressor, if we learn to pursue it with poise and with ease; it surely need not be a life-destroying force, if we learn to regulate the number of hours it must claim, and declare a daily interval between it and ourselves.

HESITATION AND DECISION

God endowed man with the powers of judgment and decision. The faculty of judgment was given to him to enable him to distinguish between the salutary and the deleterious, between the beneficial and the baleful, between that which promotes and that which hinders happiness. With his judgment man weighs and balances the advantages against the disadvantages of a situation, of a circumstance, or of an enterprise. To complement this we have the power of decision. Following the selection made by the judgment, the mind throws its entire weight on the side of the selected purpose, it identifies itself with the selected road, it seeks to actualize the selected plan or to achieve the selected task. This is what we mean by decision. No matter what other possibilities, what other goals, had presented themselves before judgment made its choice, now that the road has been selected, the other alternatives are entirely withdrawn as if they had never existed. The entire man acts in harmony only with the chosen purpose in view. Decision, then, means that the mind has placed its signature to a definite mode of procedure, that it has subscribed to the attainment of a specific purpose, that it has bound itself to carry out a specific plan.

Hesitation, on the other hand, implies that the power of judgment is unable to make a selection. It means that where there are several circumstances, or several goals or methods to select from, the mind discerns reasons of equal validity or equal advantage in each of these and is therefore unable to choose one above the others; or it means that where there is only one purpose or one goal to be attained, the difficulty or difficulties which the attainment involves appear too great or too overwhelming, and the mind vacillates between whether or not it should act, whether or not it should venture, whether or not it should make the effort in the face of these obstacles, whether or not it should expose itself to threatening hardships in order to reach the goal. These, then, are the two possible kinds of hesitation; one in which the judgment is unable to choose because there are several possibilities to choose from; the other, in which it is unable to decide even when only one possibility is involved, because of pre-conceived impediments connected with its realization.

Of the first kind of indecision let me say that the mind must compel itself to find advantages in following one road above other possible roads. The fact that there are several roads, several possibilities to choose from, means naturally that each of these is possessed of qualities and advantages which the others are denied. If each one of the alternatives is possessed of distinct advantages and disadvantages, if each of these has its own inviting and repelling aspects, then an individual must be able to say to himself: I shall choose *this* and not *that*; I shall make this my goal and shall let all the others go; I shall employ this as my method and not all these others; I shall follow this and not the other as my ideal. If an individual cannot choose one road from many roads, or one goal from many goals, or one possibility from a variety of possibilities, it is either because he is mentally ill, or because he is cowardly. I say he may be mentally ill; for when different situations and different projects and different ends appear of equal value so that no selection can be made, a condition exists very similar analogically to a case of tactile insensibility where the individual is unable to distinguish between the objects he touches, or to a case of color blindness where one cannot distinguish between colors, or to a case of aphasia where one is incapable of distinguishing between the sounds he hears. Here, too, his power of judgment is impaired, and he is therefore unable to make a selection, all possibilities appearing the same to him. On the other hand, as I have said, he may be unable to decide simply because he is cowardly. He discerns differences, he sees quite well the advantages and the disadvantages of each possibility, but he dares not choose one and discard the others, lest the rejected ones prove in the end more advantageous. These are the people who would like always to do the things which they did not do, and when they indeed attempt to do that which they had first rejected, they soon discover that not that either, but that which they had first attempted and dropped was after all the better thing for them.

An individual must be able to decide for himself what is advantageous and what is disadvantageous, what is good and what is bad, what is wholesome and what is injurious to his existence. A man must have a definite *yes* and a definite *no*. He must be able to say *no* with just as much emphasis as he says *yes*. As to those things which he excludes from his life, it is just as essential to his well being that he exclude them as it is essential to his well being to include certain other things. If his deciding faculty be weak, let it be strengthened; if it be cowardly, let it be recharged with courage; if it be sick, let it be cured. But how? Simply this: if all vocations appear alike, if all ideals bear the same color, all methods the same tone, let him choose the first one that appears desirable; let him follow his first judgment, let him decide on his first selection, let him attempt to reach the first goal that appealed to him, and let him act energetically, and with great determination and effort, to carry out that first choice. That first is his and all the other possibilities must be rejected, and annihilated from memory. They must not be shown any recognition or given opportunity to present themselves again, for if they do, they will claim attention and energy, and will again cause doubt and hesitancy.

I said that indecision may manifest itself either where one choice is to be made out of many given situations, or where only one situation presents itself, the execution of which is, however, surrounded with difficulties. The individual in that latter case is in a state of hesitancy as to whether or not he shall make the effort to undertake its realization.

Let it be clear that we do not indentify hesitation with deliberation. Deliberation is the natural process of weighing and balancing benefits against difficulties, gain against hardships, results against efforts. It is a process of circumspection and forethought; but deliberation is always followed by a firm decision. The individual emerges from clouds into light, from uncertainty into conviction, and his acts follow the course of his decision. In hesitancy there is apparently the method of deliberation, but not its probing process nor its search for a definite conclusion. This hesitancy is strictly an offspring of cowardice. It seeks shelter under the mantle of reflection and deliberation, it takes on the appearance of thought and foresight but is in reality fearful of any venture lest it may have to cope with hardships and privation. The mind hesitates; this means that it is perfectly willing to remain at a standstill rather than take a hazardous step.

Let me say to these hesitating minds, that to every individual there come moments for decision; these are often the great moments in one's life; they frequently seal one's fortune, they often hold the key to one's happiness. If one loses these moments he may be denying himself the benefits of advancement, the satisfaction of attainment, the joy of self-development and self-elevation.   This is what we mean by opportunity. Opportunity is not the finding of abundance upon our threshold; it is not the picking up of a fortune lying right before our eyes; it is not the unexpected turn of the wheel of destiny; opportunity is the firm decision one makes at the great moments of his life, it is the pursuance with vigor and energy and enthusiasm of that which one has set out to do, it is the unhesitating, unbending, unswerving attitude towards that which one regards as right and beneficial.

It is curious that when one decides to do something and begins to do it he immediately discovers that the task is not so difficult as he first imagined it to be, that the obstacles are not so stubborn, that the burdens are not so heavy, that the impediments are not so insurmountable as they first appeared to be. From a distance a duty shows itself in exaggerated dimensions, appears of extravagant weight, of gigantic pressure; this distance between the individual and the duty he perceives is usually filled up with a mist, and through the mist, figures are blurred and distorted, and give rise to threatening, fantastic images. But when the individual comes nearer to his duty, these distortions disappear. As soon as the individual lays hold upon reality, discouraging imaginings find no room in his mind. Therefore, decide and begin, and half of the work is done; the remaining half will be the easier one.

We know that the world is possessed of far greater treasures than those which man has so far discovered. There is more gold, more "acres of diamonds" in the earth than man has yet unearthed. There is more fertility, more productiveness in the soil than man has yet brought forth. The field can yield far more grain than it does, the fruit tree can bear more fruit, and man too can think and create far more than he hitherto has. There is tragedy in the waste of the soil, but there is infinitely greater tragedy in the wastage of human energy, thought and life. Hesitation is the great destroyer of human power. You can achieve great things in life, why, then, hesitate? You can grow and expand and prosper, why, then, hesitate? You can make a masterpiece of your life, you can build yourself an immortal spiritual monument, why, then, hesitate? You can, through your efforts, help to make the world better, finer, nobler, why, then, hesitate?

What would have happened to mankind if its great seers and leaders and thinkers had hesitated? What would have happened to mankind if Moses had hesitated before he ascended the Mount? If Isaiah had hesitated in uttering his prophecies? If Jeremiah had hesitated before a hostile world? Come down with me to a later age. What would have happened if Galileo had hesitated, if Columbus had hesitated, if Fulton had hesitated? If these minds had hesitated the world today would have been behind by at least two thousand years. Each one who hesitates retards the world, hinders progress, holds back civilization. Each one who lives a life of decision and achievement advances the world, contributes to civilization and is a blessing to mankind.

CONCERNING SENSITIVENESS

Man is by nature a sensitive being. I am using the term sensitive here in its broad sense. I mean that man, through his nervous system, through his sensory mechanism, becomes the recipient of influences in his environment. He is first the receiver of atmospheric influences; he is sensitive to cold, to heat, to wind and to shower. Then he is sensitive to appearances in the surroundings in which he is placed: to chaos, to disharmony, to ugliness, as well as to order, to symmetry and to beauty. It is here, we may say, that we can detect the unique gift of the poet. The poet is particularly sensitive to the exquisite, the harmonious in nature, and this discernment yields him intense pleasure and delight. While the average individual sees the beautiful and appreciates it, the poet more than sees it, he absorbs it with all the might of his soul, and strives to identify himself with it. Man is also sensitive to the mood and attitude of his fellow man. He responds to the cheerfulness or the gloom of the one who is with him, to his irritability or to his peaceableness, to his intensity or his serenity, to his love or his bitterness. Man is sensitive also to praise and blame. In this specific application, the term sensitiveness is attached to men and women whose feelings are particularly vulnerable, whose sense of pride is easily wounded, who become vehemently aroused or who morbidly withdraw into themselves at the slightest suspicion of a slight. We shall concern ourselves here with this weakness on the part of humankind.

There are many in this world who are too finely sensitized to the moods and attitudes of others, who are too greatly dependent for their happiness upon the good opinion of their neighbors. These are the men and women who look upon themselves always through the eyes of others. Over-sensitiveness to the opinion of other people is a detriment which is responsible for many unhappy hours in life. I do not mean to underestimate the value of social regard and opinion. We are indeed social beings, we live in the midst of the group, we are guided by its standards, we conduct ourselves in accordance with its judgments, we follow its

regulations and identify ourselves with its
ideals, and it is but natural that we should
cherish its praise and value its approval.
But there is a wide difference between following society, complying with its highest
standards and thereby gaining the prize of
its approval, on the one hand, and, on the
other hand, seeking consciously and eagerly
its adulation and applause as ends in themselves. Those who do not seek praise but who
gain it because of acts that spontaneously call
forth praise, are, as a rule, the masters of
society; while those who primarily seek the
praise of society and are dependent upon it
for their happiness are the slaves of society.

Man has a right to desire respect, but he
must not seek it for its own sake. He who
goes out in quest of it will not find it, he who
sets his heart upon obtaining it will meet with
disappointment. Esteem, honor, respect, are
things which must come to man indirectly, a
natural compensation for acts which deserve
esteem, honor, and respect. To be over-desirous
of this good opinion, to deliberately seek it, to
be sensitive to its withholding, is to surrender
one's freedom and individual judgment.

To be over-sensitive to praise, however, is no more culpable than to be over-sensitive to reproach or blame. These men and women who are so easily hurt, whose feelings are instantly wounded, who are too ready to perceive a slight, these men and women may be very good people, they may be the possessors of high characters, but in their sensitiveness to reproach, in their anxiety over a discrimination or a slight, they are doing themselves and others a grave injury. Those who are sensitive to injury will find themselves hurt, even where injury was never intended or offered. Those who are over-sensitive to insult will detect it even where only friendliness and goodwill exist, until their relations with others become a tangled web of misunderstanding and misjudgment. Such a tendency stirs up noxious reactions, and may create bitterness and animosity, where only amity should have existed.

Here we can see how enemies may be made. The natural relation between human beings is that of friendship and good-will. Bring children together and you will find that they will attract, not repel one another; they will play together, they will laugh together, they will grow enthusiastic and joyful over some joint project or other. Bring mature people together, and if they are not hampered by ceremony and convention, you will observe that their spirits, too, will become animated, their thought stimulated, their whole personality enhanced by pleasant communion with their kind. The social instinct is, indeed, a powerful factor in human life. What is it, then, that creates animosity and estrangement? It is, as a rule, oversensitiveness, which leads to misunderstanding. When men and women are so high-strung and self-absorbed that they are constantly on the alert for some injury to their pride, they will misinterpret the speech, misjudge the gestures, misconstrue the motives and conduct of even their dearest friends. This will create hatred and bitterness in them, and in turn generate the same emotions in others.

We learn, in Jewish Science, always to look upon the sunny aspect of life, never to deliver ourselves to tendencies of gloom and depression, nor steep ourselves in sadness, nor let pessimism possess our being; these are states of being not intended by divine creation, they are human acquisitions, which man himself has developed in error and to his own detriment. To look upon the bright side of life means also to look upon the bright side of our fellow-man, it means to interpret him and his actions and his motives in a favorable light. True kindness does not mean doing a kindness for a kindness, it does not mean doing a favor for a favor, or a sacrifice for a sacrifice made. That is nothing more than the payment of a debt, a debt of honor. True kindness is manifested in a kindly construction of a fellow-man's motives and acts. And should a fellow-being prove himself utterly unworthy of such an interpretation, then there is opportunity for the exercise of magnanimity. There are moments in man's life which are marked by supreme nobility, and these are the moments when he refuses to take notice of an unkindness, when he refuses to hear words of unfriendliness, above all, when he refuses to harbor a grudge for an insult offered or an injustice done him. At such moments, man stands at the top of his manhood.

Sensitiveness is, in many instances, allied with self-centeredness. The individual who does not center his mind on himself, who does not think constantly of himself, who does not watch closely his own moods or his own feelings or his own reactions, will not suffer from the tortures of sensitiveness. And self-centeredness is not necessarily selfishness; it is a disproportionate interest in the self, due sometimes to the mere fact that the individual has nothing else in which to center his interest. Let him shift his center of interest, let him identify himself with some task, particularly let him identify his life with an ideal, and his sensitiveness will assuredly be banished. For he will then think of his tasks, and delight in his ideal and labor for it, and things pertaining to his own person will become insignificant, hurts that touch his own being will lose their sting, they will not exist.

OVERCOMING INDOLENCE

Success has frequently been identified in people's minds with luck or chance. We all know those grumblers against fate who palliate their failure with some such sentiments: "Oh, if I had his luck, I would have done as well as he, or better." "If I had had his chance, I would also have been successful." Yet a little observation would reveal to these men that, if there is such a thing as luck in life, it seems always to accompany the steps of the industrious and the diligent; while it makes a wide detour to avoid meeting the indolent.

We do not believe in good luck or in bad luck; we know that so-called good luck is not a cause, but a result—the result of effort and labor; and bad luck is not a cause, it is the consequence of laziness and indifference to one's task. The industrious man has good fortune constantly at his heels; the indolent man, somehow, is constantly shadowed by an opposite fate. This world of ours is based entirely on cause and effect, and the effect is always

commensurate with the cause. A man's success in life is entirely the result of his industry
or self-application to his life's calling.

God did not create luck, but he created man
fully equipped with powers and facilities for
the achievement of success. He has given him
hands with which to work, eyes with which to
see, ears with which to hear. Above all, He
has endowed him with a mind, with which to
think and plan, and design his own future.
But these tools of achievement are handed
over to man's will. He may do with them
whatever he chooses. He may utilize them
constantly to attain his ends, and receive inevitable compensation. Or he may, if he will, let
them exist in an inactive state, so that in time
his faculties will rust and atrophy; and the
consequence of such disuse of his God-given
powers is poverty,—material or spiritual,—
and unhappiness.

Indolence is not a disease; it is a sin. It is
not to be confused with that nervous mental
ailment in which the patient, overwhelmed by a
sense of fatigue and nerve exhaustion, is unable to make even the slightest exertion. Such
an ailment can be healed, in the same way

that other ailments are healed. But indolence is not an ailment, it needs no healer; it is a sin, and the individual himself must cleanse himself of it. Indolence is not inherited, it is just a faulty habit of living. It means that the will was not brought into action in the early stages of life, and that life, therefore, has remained stagnant. But it is a state from which one can free himself, if he will; and free himself simply by acquiring the opposite habit of industry.

One does not really count in the world of men until he has done something useful. An individual stands for that which he achieves; his achievement is a monument to his personality. And a man must seek to express his individuality in some specific task which should happily engage and utilize all his powers. When a man finds himself fettered by the chains of indolence, watching the days fleeting by and leaving no trace or shadow of their presence in his individual life, then his days do not count at all in the making of the world.

Many of us, perhaps, know of the happiness that is gained through benevolence, through kindness, through love; and that is a high type of happiness indeed. But among the keenest, the most poignant happiness that man can know is that which comes from the sense of achievement. The joy of work is among our most blessed experiences. He who labors and achieves may well have the satisfaction of feeling that he is contributing his share to the progress of mankind, to the completion of the world. He knows that whatever he gets from life is in compensation for what he gives to life. He may look upon his home and rightly say, "this is the compensation for my share of work to mankind"; he may look upon his grounds, his possessions, his fortunes, and rightly say: "these are the rewards of my toil; this is the exchange for my thought, for my enterprise, for my industry, for what I give of myself to mankind." On the other hand, the one who saunters through life without contributing anything of himself to the world, does not truly enjoy the happiness that life offers. Life to him is always empty, days are but a procession of unsubstantial shadows, which come and go, leaving no mark upon him. Whatever he gets from life, though he may have plenty, is in the form of alms, for he gives nothing for what he receives from life. To the idle or indolent man life then becomes miserable, often intolerable, and he may even ask himself whether life is worth living.

The industrious man never harbors pessimistic thoughts; the joy of self-expression is his and leaves no room for a gloomy outlook. It is the man steeped in habitual indolence who most often shelters depression and doubt. The man of industry does not fear hardship and drudgery, for he knows that the easiest way of overcoming them is not by slothfully avoiding them, but by meeting them face to face and conquering them step by step. The diligent man holds a most effective weapon in his hand —his will to work, and his ability to enjoy his work—and armed with this, he is safe from fear and failure. It is the man dragged down by indolence who finds himself helpless in this world, and open to the attacks of depressing and fearful thoughts.

The worst of the many evils of indolence is its deteriorating effect upon man. The human mind, as we know, is so constituted that it can never remain at a standstill; it must move forward, if not, it will move backward. It either gains in power and velocity, or it deteriorates in capacity and quality. When the mind becomes flabby, the flesh becomes flabby, when the mind becomes weak, the body becomes feeble. We often hear admonitions against overwork, against the dangers that long hours of toil may bring. And it is true that excess is not desirable even in a good direction. But much should also be said about the dangers of underwork, about the many ailments which follow days upon days of laziness.

Where indolence has taken root, may it be eradicated? The answer is obvious. There would be no need to dwell on the ravages of indolence, if it were impossible to banish it. The process, in fact, is very simple. It requires but an earnest desire and a strong initial effort. You may say, those of you who are suffering from the habit of inertness, that you have already made many efforts, but that after every spurt of activity, degrading indolence falls upon you once more. It is possible that your efforts have missed the right direction. Let me point out first of all what not to do, and then lay out certain simple steps to follow. Do not proceed to change your entire being in one day; if you think you can achieve this, you will without doubt meet with disappointment. Do not decide to become industrious for the rest of your life; you will not succeed by merely making that decision. The mind may decide it, but the limbs and the muscles which have been dormant for years, may refuse to obey the decision. To bring yourself from indolence to industry means to re-educate your entire system. Above all, it is the will that is to perform the entire task of re-education, and in the habit of indolence it is the will that is flabby and unable to stir. Adopt therefore the following method: determine to spend *one* industrious day. Do not plan ahead of that day. Decide upon something useful to do to-morrow, just to-morrow, and do it. You can be industrious for one day. Do not speak to anyone of your struggles with yourself and of the conquest that you are going to make. By speaking of it in advance, by priding yourself on what you are going to do, you are wasting your will and your imagination. And when these are wasted, you have little left to proceed with. Whatever changes you desire to make in your soul, do it silently without words. Decide then, to be industrious for one day, and in this, without doubt, you will succeed. When that day is over, determine to spend the very next day in the same industrious fashion. And again do not plan beyond that particular day. Continue this process for fourteen successive days, and you will find your forces of industry so strongly advanced that you will not be able to suppress them. You will find yourself compelled to do something useful every day; you will find it easier to be diligent than to be slothful. And during these fourteen days, and ever after, you will discover a new source of joy— the joy of achievement.

There is another implement that you should use to lift yourself from the morass of indolence, and that is affirmative prayer. God, we have said before, has endowed man with the power to think and to plan; He has, in His great love, endowed him also with a heart with which to pray—to ask for help when his own powers are unable to attain his goal. Prayer is efficacious not only for health, but for every deficiency and deformity in human nature. One who is desirous of lifting himself from indolence, must, in addition to his own efforts, seek for help from a higher source. He must pray for it; and that help will never fail him. He must affirm with his whole heart: "The God consciousness in me expresses itself in diligence and in achievement." Let him repeat this affirmation twice each day, morning and evening, and he will successfully evoke the Divine help for his efforts in achieving the godlike virtue of industry.

SELF-MASTERY

The Talmud, endeavoring to define heroism, arrives at the conclusion that true heroism lies in self-conquest. "Who is a hero?" the sage of the Talmud inquires. And the answer is, "A hero is he who masters himself." This is truly an unusual definition of heroism. Heroism is associated in our minds with feats of valor, with triumph on fields of battle, with the annihilation of armies, with the capture of cities, with superhuman effort or endurance in resisting onslaught or overcoming resistance. Here we read of a new kind of heroism,—the heroism involved in self-mastery. If this task were an easy one, if one were able to do what he ought without hindrance and with little effort, then the conqueror of the self would not be termed a hero; heroism, without exception, involves a struggle; a hero, always, is one who conquers, who vanquishes someone or something, and the greater the struggle, the greater the triumph, the greater the glory of the conqueror.

Now, in the mastery of the self, what is it that man really conquers? Before we answer this question, we must first take a glimpse into the contents of man's nature, and see what therein is to be regarded as inimical and detrimental to man's well-being, and therefore to be subdued or annihilated.

Man possesses in his make-up two kinds of reactions; one is positive and the other is negative, one is a divine endowment, the other is a human development, one seeks to preserve man, while the other is indifferent to man's preservation. We therefore frequently find man in opposite moods, his mind moving in opposite states, his heart straining in conflicting directions. Every tendency of man, whether native or acquired, has a will of its own, a potency of its own, and a deep craving to find expression *through* man. Man, then, becomes a tool in the hands of conflicting proclivities; when one tendency acquires a hold upon his consciousness, he lends himself to it, when another, a stronger tendency, grasps him, he naturally gives himself to it in turn, swaying thus from one inner hold to another. Self-mastery means this: that instead of lending himself as a servant or as a slave to every strong desire that wells from within, man suppresses the harmful tendencies in his being and allows them no expression. And not only does he fortify himself against them, but he musters the courage and persistence to fight them and extirpate them. It is the one who courageously struggles against noxious tendencies and reactions within himself and triumphs over them, it is he whom the sage calls a hero—a man who has mastered himself.

What are some of the weaknesses in man's disposition which should be fought and eradicated? There is, to begin with, anger, which is an exceedingly bitter foe of man, which ravages man, which weakens him and poisons the vital essence of his being. Anger destroys the angry; it fills their heart with ever-recurring bitterness, and their minds with constant resentment. Those who give themselves over to anger always see before them a provoking world, they always find themselves in an irritating atmosphere; all circumstances,—strangers, friends, even the elements,—all conspire to feed their irate temper and make their life miserable. Anger saps man's vitality, it constantly diminishes his strength; a constant outpour of anger is a constant outpour of energy. The harm anger does to a man, his bitterest enemy cannot possibly bring about.

Let me mention another inimical tendency in man—fear. Fear is unlike anger. Those who are mastered by anger assume a belligerent attitude, they are always ready to strike someone or something; those who are overcome with fear show a cowering attitude, they shrink from everyone and from everything. They are always anticipating some dread thing that may happen, something dangerous and injurious that may take place. Fear keeps man down, it holds him imprisoned, it invests everyone he meets with inimical power, it permeates the atmosphere with threat and foreboding. Fear is a dangerous influence, it retards man's energies, it holds back man's creative powers, it puts chains on man's enterprising impulses, it stunts man's growth and blocks his development; it must be eradicated from the heart of man.

Then there is hatred—another base tendency in the mind of man. Hatred again differs from fear; fear makes man retreat, hatred does not.

Hatred also differs from anger; anger occupies the foreground in the human personality, while hate usually occupies the background. Anger shows itself, expresses itself; hatred can hide itself, it can disguise itself, dissemble itself. Hatred finds its origin in the inability to condone a wrong, in the inability to overlook, in the stringent demand of righteousness from others, but not from oneself. Hatred, too, is destructive to man. Aside from its violation of the most sacred human ethics, it proves most noxious to the mind in which it dwells. Hatred makes man critical, it makes man carping and cynical, it takes the gist and the joy out of life. For the happiness of man, it must be fought and vanquished.

But how is one to battle and uproot deep-seated tendencies and moods which have been with one, perhaps for many years? In the first place, one must recognize his own failings. Without this recognition, self-help is impossible. Then proceed to check these weaknesses by conscious resistance, and by invocation of divine help. Refuse to lend yourself to anger. When you feel it coming, surging in your heart, charging your tongue, filling your eyes, refuse it passage through your being, refuse to make yourself a tool for its expression. When in anger, refuse to speak, refuse to write, refuse to act until the storm subsides and you are yourself again. When in anger, keep the chamber of your energies locked, your senses numb, your faculties silent. Remember that anger is a pugnacious agent. Fear, on the other hand, is a cringing impulse; proceed, therefore, in the very opposite direction. Insist on facing the thing you fear, on doing the things you fear, on understanding, on realizing the facts you dread. Do not keep in the rear, do not keep in concealment, force yourself to act. If you wish to eradicate hatred from your soul, insist on putting a kindly interpretation on the acts and deeds of those who are the object of your hate, standing for a moment in their place, taking into consideration their training, their circumstances, their position. This is what we mean by conscious resistance.

To support this battle with yourself, invoke the help of the Divine Mind. In Jewish Science, we find that divine help is not a myth, it is a reality. We, in Jewish Science, experience divine help every day, and therefore seek divine help in all our difficulties, in all our hardships. In this particular problem of self-mastery, you will find the affirmative prayer of the greatest efficacy, for it will help you to fight anger with serenity, fear with courage, hatred with love. When you feel anger overcoming you, affirm: "The God-consciousness in me expresses itself in serenity and in peace." If fear possesses your being, affirm: "The God-consciousness in me expresses itself in courage and in strength." If you are about to succumb to the emotion of hatred, affirm: "The God-consciousness in me expresses itself in sympathy and in love." And, you will find, these prayers are unfailingly answered.

Self-conquest, we must realize, is the greatest of all conquests. Self-conquest is true heroism. One may be master of many enterprises, he may be master over circumstances, he may be master of wisdom and of knowledge, he may be master even of others, but if he is not master of himself, he is really a slave. The most precious power is the power over oneself, the finest achievement is the mastery of the self.

CONCERNING FEAR

Fear first entered the human heart when man became conscious of the overwhelming forces of nature, of their spontaneous outbursts, of their mighty, irresistible action. His understanding as yet uncultivated, his mind undeveloped, the laws of God in nature were entirely unknown to him. Therefore, in his want of knowledge, in his great mental darkness, a terrifying emotional reaction took possession of him, and lodged itself in his being. The law behind the rolling thunder, behind the flash of lightning, not being within the grasp of his intelligence, he gave instead free play to his imagination, and created, behind the sweeping forces of nature, wrathful deities, destructive spirits, who filled him only with fear and horror.

In man's struggle for existence, too, fear played an emphatic role. Before man relinquished his cave in forest and field and learned to build himself a home that was safe from the attack of the savage beasts and still fiercer elements, he was in constant dread of these marauders. Fear took still deeper lodgment in man's consciousness when, later, living in groups, his ignorance of a sanitary mode of living, brought upon him plague and pestilence.

Thus, fear took a persistent stand in human consciousness, it dug a deep channel in the human heart, it entrenched itself in the human mind. And to-day, after the lapse of thousands and thousands of years, man is still in the terrible possession of fear. Man to-day has no cause to fear the elements, for he has discovered their laws, and understands how to protect himself from them. He has no cause to fear the ferocity of wild beasts, or the ravages of plagues, for these too he has completely banished from his midst. Man's fears, however, have only changed their object; the fears still persist. The situation is a strange and unhappy one. We see man risen from the lower to the higher, from ignorance to knowledge, from darkness to wisdom; we see him delving into the heart of nature, unraveling its mysteries, revealing its treasures, mastering its laws; we see him a strong and powerful fig-

ure, the climax of creation. Yet he is still a
victim to fear, cowering and helpless before
the agonies of his imagination. What a contrast does he present! Here he is a master
and there he is a slave; here he is a hero, and
there he is dismayed; here he is a conqueror
and there he is subdued—a prisoner to his
own fears. Man's intellect has grown, but his
courage has made no progress; his ignorance
has been conquered, but his fears still hold
sway. Man's fears have been transferred from
primitive objects, but they are still powerfully
active. And they exert themselves, for the
most part, in three definite directions. The
man of to-day fears poverty, fears sickness,
and fears public opinion.

The aspect of this subjection to fear is all
the more tragic in that all these fears are
groundless. Man has no cause to fear poverty.
Poverty is not the law of God. God created
abundance and plenty. He supplied sustenance
for all his creatures; this means, that even
long before they are called into existence, their
provisions are prepared for them. God replen-
ishes the resources of nature; the earth is

constantly yielding its riches and its treasures. There is more growth, more supply at every season than man can possibly consume. There is abundance in nature, and that which is found in nature belongs to man. Only, man must make the effort to reach out for it, he must toil for it, he must labor in one direction or another to obtain it. The more one makes the effort, the more does he insure himself against poverty. The more one utilizes his energies constructively, the more one brings his vision, his judgment, his creative ability into action, the more may he rest assured that he will receive his share of God's supply. In order that man may not remain an uncultivated being, it was God's design not to bring man his supply to his threshold. Such a process would have doomed man to perpetual indolence, to ignorance and darkness. It would have held man down to a primitive, undeveloped existence. God, for man's own good, did not place man's food ready at his door, but made it necessary for him to reach out, to search for it; and during his search, during his labor for the attainment of sustenance, his faculties unfold themselves, his powers gain in keenness and in potency, his manhood asserts itself and he grows in stature with his gains. Only the fear of poverty makes poverty possible. The fear of poverty discourages a man's ambitions, it blurs his energies, and with his powers thus out of action, want may actually knock at his door. It is the fear of poverty that one must combat and annihilate, and when this enemy within is exterminated, man, with his labors, will always find food and shelter; and when he finds these two, he is not poor.

Nor should man fear sickness, for sickness, too, is not the creation of God. God created health, strength, energy, power, but not sickness. Man is born to be healthy and vigorous; he himself is responsible for his sickness. God supplies man with health, but this is an exceedingly valuable treasure, man must use it judiciously. He must use it with utmost care and conservation. I know men and women who are economical with their wealth, yet how extravagant they are with their health. Health is an invisible treasure given to man for use but not for waste, for achievement, not for dissipation, for happiness, not for devastation. Health is a delicate, though most precious, jewel; it can be hurt in many ways. Excessive drudgery on one's part will weaken it; constant hurry will undermine it; bitterness, irritation, anger will injure it; worry will destroy it. All influences that are noxious or strenuous to the mind will leave its mark upon the health; man, through his irregularity of living, through his unremittent excitement, makes an aperture through which health escapes and sickness enters.

The fear of sickness is itself an invitation to sickness. The more one fears ailment the more does he expose himself to it. The fear of sickness brings on sleeplessness, it brings on disturbances in the digestive processes. The fear of sickness weakens and slackens the heart beats and causes depression in the respiratory organs. The individual will then actually find himself ill, and it will be illness caused greatly by his mere fear. The less man fears sickness, the more will he prevent it and the more surely will he ward it off. In all illnesses, moreover, the state of mind of the patient is of great moment. When the mind is full of cheer and hope and faith, restoration is far easier. But when the mind is filled with fear, stricken with terror, recovery becomes a difficult and prolonged task. There is no reason to fear sickness, as there is no reason to fear poverty. God is the source of health, the sustainer of life, the restorer of strength, why then fear? Use your health aright, use it wisely, and economically, trust in God and seek His protection, and nothing will assail your strength.

Another cause of misery to-day is the dominant tendency to cower before public opinion. Man in our civilized society today is an utter slave to public opinion. The question paramount in his mind seems constantly to be: What will his neighbors think of him? How will his acts appear to the eyes of others? Men and women will disguise themselves, will hide their real selves, conceal their natural individuality, in order to gain the good opinion of their neighbors. They will go hungry and appear feasted, they will sink deeper into debt and appear wealthy, they will deny themselves bread in order to adorn themselves with jewels that they may gain the approving opinion of their neighbors. And their neighbors do the same things in order to win *their* favor. This is an arbitrary, artificial and ruinous mode of life.

Why should civilized men and women look upon themselves through the eyes of others? Why should they seek to *appear* rather than *to be?* Why not be themselves, why not give expression to their genuine selves in every walk of life? When their true, deep self is made manifest, they will find that there is much refinement in their nature and they need not imitate it, that there is true nobility in their spirit and they need not imitate it, that there is tenderness and goodness and grace in their own heart and they need not imitate these. When man expresses his true divine self, he need not fear, he has no cause to fear, the opinion of his fellow-men.

In civilized life there is no cause at all for fear. Poverty, illness and public opinion, when correctly analyzed, can have no terror for us. We are endowed with courage, with optimism, with power; let these virtues of our finer selves find full expression through us, and all our fears will vanish.

YOUNG AT SEVENTY

Resignation always marks a weakness in human character. Whenever a man resigns himself to a condition or circumstance, he thereby declares his unwillingness or inability to stand up and battle with it. In resignation, man surrenders his self-confidence, his self-mastery, his self-assertion. This holds true in any case of surrender, whether it be a battle with a foe, or a struggle against unfavorable circumstances, or the acceptance of debility and feebleness as the accompaniment of old age. It is in this latter form of surrender that we are interested at this moment.

It is customary for a man of seventy to feel old, to see himself on the downward slope of life, to anticipate weakness and restlessness and inactivity, to become irritable and discontented, to look with longing eyes upon the past and to face the future with foreboding or resignation. At seventy we are accustomed to see many clouds in the sun, much dreariness in the atmosphere, much weariness in nature. At seventy, we see but little of the cheerful side of life, our sense of humor is inactive, our laughter almost frozen. At that period we feel that our work is already achieved, our tasks already done, and that it is time for us to retire into quietude, giving up our place to others. No wonder, then, that advanced age, though deeply respected and revered, is regarded by many as not an ideal stage of life.

It is our belief, in Jewish Science, that the unpleasantness and unhappiness experienced in old age is not due to a divine law set in man, but to the erroneous opinions man fosters of himself. It is due to his misconception of the significance of years, to his misapprehension of age and of time. Years are not God's creation, they are man's invention. A year is a human measure of time; it is man's yardstick by which he determines duration, but it is not God's criterion by which life is checked off. This truth, though elementary, it is extremely essential to know, for it means that God does not count the years, that He does not number man's days, that He does not measure life by arbitrary human standards. The age of seventy, therefore, is not necessarily a landmark of old age; it is not necessarily a signal to all the traditional weaknesses of old age to come and invade the human form and make their abode therein; it is not necessarily an entrance into a state of infirmity and decrepitude. Life at seventy may be a continuation of power and vigor and well-being.

What are the outstanding differences between youth and advanced age? Youth is aspiring and ambitious, youth is optimistic and hopeful, youth is vigorous and powerful. All these things advanced age apparently is not. Now, why is youth optimistic and ambitious and self-assertive? It is because, at that stage, man realizes that he is here to build his world, to improve himself and his opportunities, to make a conquest of life. In his youth, man sees the world before him, not behind him; the horizon to him is then very distant and endless. This is not the case in advanced age. Man then feels that his achievements are completed, his conquests made; there is nothing left for him but to wait for the end of his days.

With such an outlook upon life, there can be
no inspiration, no ambition, no action and no
hope. It is not, however, *inherent* in the nature
of man to grow resigned and pessimistic with
the advent of the years. It is his accepted conception of age that renders him so. If pessimism and resignation were linked with advanced years just as thought is with the mind
or vision with the eye, if it were as inevitable
as the night following the day, then man would
of necessity need to submit to his destiny.
But since this mood is but the result of man's
misconception of the years, it is his conception
that must be changed and a new attitude implanted. Then the dour atmosphere that hangs
about old age will vanish of itself.

There is no reason why a man of seventy
should see his work as already done. No work
in reality is ever completed—be it a man's
private enterprise or be it his labors in the
field of benevolence, or of spiritual advancement or of self-improvement. In private enterprise, if he is successful, his vision is surely
open to more expansion, more enlargement,
more growth; if not successful, he can surely

not afford to stop; he must make more effort, call more thought and experience into action, until victory is won. It is needless to point out that in the field of benevolence, or spiritual advancement, or self-improvement, man's work cannot ever be completed; for these are endless necessities and endless privileges, and therefore endless tasks. Whether a man is seventy or more than seventy, his work is never finished. And he must not view his life in terms of wealth and possessions. In terms of possession, he may find himself well provided for, with no necessity for further effort. But measuring life in terms of achievement, he can never retire, for his tasks need him more and more.

We therefore say that no man, in his advanced years, should retire from responsibility, from achievement, or from advancement. As an excellent tonic, a man in his advanced years should seek and hold on to an ideal, identify himself with it, make it his own. He should foster it, cherish it, nurture it and advance it; the more he does this, the more does he cast off from himself the burden of days and the heaviness of years. By identifying himself with an ideal, man's soul energy is brought into action, and the body will cease to claim weakness and infirmity. For it is in the nature of the body to serve as a tool, to be an implement in the hand of some aspiration or goal, and when such a mission is denied it, it begins to weaken and deteriorate. The flesh is like iron; if it is not employed, it will rust and lose its strength. Man, by making himself servant to an ideal, will find his aspiration growing stronger, his optimism growing deeper, his hopes expanding, and the chief difference between his advanced days and his youthful days will be obliterated. He will be recharged with energy, his heart will keep young.

If you will contend that man is naturally weaker in his advanced years than he is in his youthful years, we must point out that this condition is greatly exaggerated through man's failure to live a life of regularity and moderation. As man's days advance, his life must become more and more regular and self-restrained. Moderation is a virtue that should be practiced at all stages of life, but particularly as the summers and winters multiply. At that time, a man must consider consequences and not merely the pleasure of the moment. A man must always be moderate with his food, but particularly so when his days have attained maturity. At that time, he must watch his bites just as he watches his steps, he must withhold from hurtful food, he must eat not to satisfy his palate but to nourish his body. One bite too many is hurtful, one untimely pleasure is dangerous, excess of any kind holds a threat. But with moderation as the guide of his advancing days, a man can retain a full measure of strength and vigor throughout the whole of his lifetime.

Another secret of prolonged youth lies in the fostering of youthful thoughts. Youth is not resigned, it does not moan, it does not lament, it is not sad. Carry a youthful air and youthful thoughts, and everything within you will continue young. We study in psychology of ailments which are greatly magnified and aggravated by the imagination, and of others which are even created by the imagination. Old age is greatly a sickness of the imagination.

As a certain number of years pass, a man begins to look upon himself as an old man. He begins to identify himself, in his imagination, with advanced age. Every temporary weakness is interpreted as the work of age, every restless day as the work of age, every sleepless night as the approach of old age. The cumulative effect of these old age suggestions upon the body is extremely hurtful, for the body and all its processes and functions are subject to these suggestions; the body follows them with great fidelity and weakens under their influence; and thus the individual does actually become decrepit and feeble in his advanced years. These evil effects are not wrought by God, they are the doings of man himself.

Man, in his advanced years, must continue to build and to achieve, he must continue to plan and hope, he must, in addition, live a strictly moderate, perfectly controlled life, he must instill into himself thoughts of strength and vigor, and then—then he will be young at seventy.

RECREATION

Studying the methods of nature we find that the processes and functions of life work rhythmically. There is no continuous, uninterrupted outpouring of energy; an unintermittent flow without cessation does not exist, there is instead a rhythmical movement, which means that there is action and rest, action and rest. How does a plant grow? It grows rhythmically, it focuses in an upward direction; its energies act and pause, act and pause. A tree, a flower, a blade of grass do not attain their mature states in a continuous upward stretch, but there is a forward movement and a stop; a rise and a rest. How does the center of life work? How does the human heart act? In the very same manner as the other functions of nature. It beats; which means that it works rhythmically; it labors and rests, labors and rests. And the other organs, too, work in the very same manner, they labor and rest in rhythmic rotation. The very senses, when em-

ployed for any long period of time, require
ease and rest.

What is true of nature in general, what is
true of the natural unconscious processes within man, holds true also of man's conscious action and expression. There must be a balance
between labor and rest, between toil and recreation. The man who toils continuously, without proportionate rest or adequate recreation
is violating the law of nature, the law of God
within him. Man does not achieve, he does not
build with his spirit only. His spirit, his invisible desires, his aerial aspirations lead and
direct and urge him on, but the tangible accomplishment is attained through the physical
senses, through the limbs, through the cellular,
vascular, muscular processes,—through the
physical instruments. And these physical organs are subject to rhythmic law. The life
spent only in toil is unnatural, and that which
is unnatural is weakening and destructive.

Recreation may be divided into two classes,
active and passive. Passive recreation means
relaxation, rest and sleep. During man's hours
of labor, volumes of his energy are consumed,

cells are drained of their vitality, muscular
strength becomes reduced; through the hours
of sleep and relaxation, the reservoir of
strength becomes replenished, the cells are re-
built, the energies restored. During sleep man
becomes reborn, he actually becomes re-cre-
ated. Sleep is God's tonic to His creatures; it is
a particular boon to man. Man may have many
hardships during the day, but in his hours of
rest these hardships melt away; man may experience discouragements during the day, but
they vanish during the hours of sleep; man
may meet with disappointments during the
day, he may need to fight and struggle and
bear heavy burdens, but the strain and the
load all are eased with sleep. Sleep therefore
must be watched and provided for. One must
not labor beyond the hours of labor into the
hours of sleep. One must not seek to outdo
others by extending his hours of toil beyond
theirs. Aside from the moral issue involved, it
brings physical injury to the individual. Had
there been anyone made of different stuff from
the rest of mankind, built of superhuman substance and strength, for him these extended

hours of labor would bear perhaps justification. But man, each man, is made of the same flesh and blood, subject to the same weaknesses, prone to grow weary and jaded and exhausted; long hours of toil extended into the night become only a source of injury and unhappiness.

Not only should one not labor after the hours of labor, but he should also keep his mind off from his tasks after these hours. Man should not carry his business anxieties, his business worries or even his business schemes with him after his business is closed. In Jewish Science, we learn that man should never harbor worry or anxiety, whether in his place of business or at home, but those who have not yet mastered the Jewish Science method of living, must at least habituate themselves, train themselves, not to carry their business troubles outside the threshold of their business place. This habit of carrying your business with you all the time, this habit of carrying everywhere with you its problems and its anxieties is ruinous to rest and sleep. The mind must be prepared for rest, just as it must be prepared for work, it must be freed from all disturbing factors before it is placed in a restful position.

Again, sleep must have its hours and regularity, even as work must have its hours and regularity. Retire every night at a definite hour. Regularity is the law of nature. Man, too, for his own good, must, in this matter as in others, follow the regularity of nature and retire at a definite hour. Do not disturb the regularity of your nervous system and it will serve you faithfully.

We have said that recreation may be passive and active. Passive recreation is rest and sleep. But while man must have his definite and regular hours of rest and sleep, he cannot possibly spend all his leisure hours in sleep. Too much sleep is just as detrimental as too little. A man must therefore also engage in active recreation. Active recreation must not be of an over-exciting nature, for excitement in the evening hours is even more of a strain and more weakening than drudgery during the working hours. One should not spend, for example, the hours of every evening in exciting games of cards. We are not speaking as a fanatic, we see no harm in a social game which gives serene pleasure, but we consider the playing of cards every evening utterly injurious. At this moment, we are not touching the moral side of the issue, we are interested in the psychological effect of the card-playing habit. We have studied the effect of nightly card games upon the individual and have observed the pernicious effect it exercises upon him. Leaving the moral issue aside at present, as we have said, we shall not dilate upon the fact that constant card games have a demoralizing influence upon the player, that they set a bad example to children, that they bring the individual nearer and nearer to gambling habits; we are interested now in what it does to the mind, to the health of the passionate player. We know now enough of its influence to advise you against the habit of this form of recreation. As men and women of understanding, we must realize what is good and what is evil, what is wholesome and what is injurious to our being, and act upon that realization. Active recreation of an over-exciting nature is not wholesome and must therefore be eliminated.

What then should be the nature of our active recreation? It should be simply a change of occupation. It should be an occupation of a nature opposite to the one in which you indulge during the day. If, for instance, your day's work consists of bodily strain, of physical effort, your recreation must be of a mental nature; it must be found in fields of mental activity. If, on the other hand, your daily task is primarily of a mental nature, involving sedentary habits, your recreation must be of a physical nature, it must consist of bodily effort. It is the nature of our nervous system that when one part of man is brought into action, the other parts have an opportunity for rest and recuperation. When the body is in action, the mind is very often at rest, and, vice versa, when the mind is laboring, the body is usually inactive. In his active recreation, man must give that part in him which labored during the day, ease and repose by calling the other part into action. He must give his fatigued self an opportunity to become recreated by giving his rested self occupation.

Recreation may also take the form of an

occupation, not opposite to but different from the one which absorbs you during the day. By different we mean different in kind; the same faculties may be involved but engaged in an entirely diverse task. A man may find a great deal of recreation, after his business hours, in books, in art, in social intercourse, in the promotion of religious or benevolent endeavor. Although these too involve action on the part of the mind, yet they call to the fore mental energy of a kind entirely different from that employed in the field of business. Therefore they have the power to refresh the mind and give proper balance to its faculties.

Man's recreation is as essential to his wellbeing as his occupation, and if he will give it its due share of time and attention, he will increase his joy in life, lend poise to his mind, and symmetry to his entire disposition.

HOW THE MIND RULES

Man is composed of two distinct elements, of body and of mind. The body is built of flesh, bone and blood. These, in turn, are compounded of microscopic protoplasmic cells. The body consists of protective structures, of organs, of appendages; of vascular, muscular, and nervous systems. The mind—and I am speaking here of the human mind—is an invisible essence; it consists of faculties, of thought processes, of memory, of imagination. The mind is the center of consciousness, it is the *essence* of man.

The mind is the master of the body. The mind directs, the body serves. The mind plans, the body moves and carries these plans into reality; the mind contrives, unites and severs, organizes and dissolves, analyses and synthesizes, classifies and invents, and the body builds in visible terms that which the mind has invisibly conceived; it gives tangible, perceptible shape to the aerial creations of the mind; it gives speech to thought, and expression to imagination. The body serves as the vehicle by which the invisible within makes itself understood to the visible without.

Because the mind is master over the body, it has the power to control and regulate its tendencies and dispositions. The body has its own instinctive proclivities, it has its own reactions, its own indigenous cravings. These inclinations of the body are for the most part normal, their expression is in most instances wholesome and even vital to existence. But these same tendencies of the body are mostly impulsive and impetuous, unrestrained and rash. Left to themselves, they would go on a rampage and devastate the body; the mind therefore has been set in full charge over them to restrain them, to direct them, to control their faulty, riotous expression. The mind is thus the director of the body.

The mind determines the reactions of the body. The mood of the mind, its tone, is reflected in the body. As the mind thinks, so does the body act. When the mind is cheerful, when the mind is hopeful, the entire body becomes charged with cheer and with hope. The limbs, then, carry the body with greater freedom and with greater ease. The heart beats with joy, the organs work with joy, the tongue speaks with joy, the senses perceive with joy, all the physical processes perform their tasks with joy; joy fills every nook, every cell, every fibre in the body. The whole body echoes the state of the mind. On the other hand, if the mind is morose, if the mind is wretched or depressed, the whole body acts in tune with the mind. Misery then fills every part of the body. Every process, every function, every organ becomes depressed and disturbed. The heart-beats become weak, the digestive processes become sluggish, respiration becomes disturbed, the very senses become dim and dull and inaccurate in their function. Here again the body reflects the mood of the mind.

Likewise when the mind is serene, the body assumes its natural and proper poise. Every bodily expression is then marked by serenity; the gait, the glance, the motion, the speech, all are imbued with ease and calmness. When, on the other hand, anger or excitement grips the mind, the body becomes its tool and its mirror. You can read it in the palor of the countenance, in the quivering lips, in the fierce look, in the clenched fist, in the trembling limbs. You can find its noxious effect as well upon every process *within* the body, for here again the body reflects the state of the mind.

The absolute mastery of the mind over the body, the absolute influence which the mind exercises over the body, is a most beneficent provision. For man has the power to control the direction of his mind. Man can choose his state of mind, he can choose his thoughts, he can reason with himself and consciously banish morbid thoughts and invite happy, hopeful ones. And through his mind the body can be helped and strengthened.

Let us consider the power of the mind in a case of bodily illness. It matters not what physical agencies one may employ to regain health, the leading one of the helpful agencies is one's own mind. Let the mind look upon the sickness as transient; let the mind minimize its significance; let the mind refuse to brood over it; let the mind desist from worry over it; let

the mind refuse to harbor morbid or despondent thoughts concerning it; and, furthermore,
let the mind insist on emphasizing cheerfulness and hope, let the mind dwell on God's
help, let the mind see each day as a day nearer
to restoration, every hour as an hour nearer to
recovery, and the ailing body will quickly regain its health and strength.   For the body
follows the lead of the mind; if the mind believes that the sickly state of the body is beyond hope, if the mind is silently convinced
that recovery will not come, then recovery will
indeed be either greatly prolonged or actually
impossible to attain. In such a case, the mind
is the hindering factor, it holds back restoration, just as in the other instance, it aids and
hastens recovery.

Not only when difficulties befall the body is
one's state of mind of paramount importance,
but equally so when one encounters difficulties
and reverses in the plans and enterprises of
life. When a man loses his wealth, let us say,
he may assume the very same attitude as when
he loses his health. His mind may retain its
optimism or it may sink deeply into pessi-

mism, and the effect on his future fortunes varies diametrically with the attitude he assumes. When a man loses his money, he must forget his losses; he must consider the period of his losses as a chapter wiped out from the book of his life. His optimism must go on unimpaired, his hopeful efforts must not be interfered with. The mind must continue to think in terms of success, it must continue to plan, to reconstruct, to rebuild, to regain that which has been lost and more. The loss must be considered only one of the incidents, not one of the accidents, of life. No man should permit himself to fall under the weight of his losses; no man should ever acknowledge himself defeated, no man should consider himself a failure in life. And if a man does not consider himself defeated, if he does not look upon himself as a failure, then he really is not defeated, he really is not a failure. If his mind has not drooped, if his courage has not suffered, if his spirit has not been cast down, then he really has lost nothing. For his cretive powers will again assert themselves, his energies will again sustain him, his efforts will again cut a way. And with the old experience and the new lessons, he will reach even further distances and greater heights than ever before. It is only when, with the loss of wealth, man loses also the optimism of his mind, when, with the loss of his fortune, he loses also his hope, that the loss counts; for it is the mental gain, not the financial one, that leads to success.

Let us bear in mind, then, that we live chiefly in the mind, not in the body. Man's kingdom is in his mind, man's throne is in his mind, man's prison house is also in his mind. As long as the mind is healthy and joyful, nothing is sick, nothing is wretched, nothing else matters; as long as the mind is optimistic and courageous, no failure is possible; as long as the mind's eye is directed upward, the whole man is moving in a forward, progressive direction from which nothing can hinder him.

THE AGE OF DISCONTENT

A generation may be observed from various angles: from the angle of its mental development, that is, its progress and civilization; from the angle of its social and political organization, referring to the state of equality and democracy it has reached; or from the angle of its industrial achievements, referring to its capacity to produce the commodities and necessities of life. Then again, it may be studied from the angle of its emotional reaction to life; how much satisfaction, how much joy, how much happiness does it receive from life? Judging our own generation from these various viewpoints, we find that in the matter of progress, we have made gigantic strides; daily, new inventions are multiplying manifold the conveniences of man; new laws of nature are being constantly discovered, adding valuable treasures to the kingdom of knowledge. Our civilization today towers high above all the civilizations of previous ages. In the presence of

our civilization, even the high civilization of
Greece and Rome falls far short. In our social
and political organization, too, our advance
has been great. The caste systems of social
discrimination have been abolished, we are
realizing more and more that men are inherently equal, that the terms high and low with
reference to mankind are misapplications. It is
for this very reason that political democracy
has made such supreme conquests; the more
men become conscious of their inherent equality, the less room is there for kings and rulers
and potentates. Political democracy, therefore, in our age, has gained ascendancy
over the globe, and personal dominion of
kings and princes over a land is dwindling,
where it has not altogether disappeared,
into merely nominal power. As to industrial achievement, our generation has
reached a pinnacle that would have staggered
the conceptions and the imagination of previous ages. Our enterprises in commerce and
industry are so vast, our efforts so daring, our
reach so great, that we are actually bringing
into play all the resources of the earth. In all

these things, we have far outdistanced those
who have come before us.   But what of our
emotional reaction to life?   Is our joy in life
as great as theirs, is our contentment with life
as deep?   Here it is that we fall short.   Ours
is an age of wisdom and achievement, but also
an age of discontent.   There is discontent
among men of every station and rank and occupation.   There is discontent among the rich
as among the poor, among the powerful as
among the weak.

Discontent, in one phase of its manifestation,
is a malady of the human mind.   It makes man
restless and uneasy; it puts a cloud over sunshine, it makes the happiest day dreary; it
weakens man's powers of enjoyment, it makes
the countenance dour, the eyes gloomy; it fills
the heart with embitterment.

Discontent, however, may be of two kinds.
They may seem closely related, but are very
distinct.   One form is discontent with one's
possessions; the other is discontent with one's
attainments.   A man, in the one case, is discontented with what he has, in the other case,
with what he is.   Discontent with one's possessions originates in envy.   One begins to be dis-

satisfied with what he has the moment he begins to envy those who possess more; he begins
to disregard his own wealth the moment he
begins to look with envy on the wealth of
others; thus he stifles his own happiness by
envying the happiness of others. This form of
discontent is unwholesome and destructive. It
becomes a morbidity, it becomes a sickness, it
becomes a source of ever-renewed distress and
misery.

This form of discontent is a state of feeling
basically unnatural to man. The natural state
is a state of contentment. That is why contentment is the true source of riches. What
matters it how abundantly one is supplied with
wealth, what matters it how many treasures he
has in his hands, what matters it if he has
jewels and gold and a sumptuous home,—if he
is discontented, his treasures will give him no
pleasure, his home will yield him no comfort,
his precious stones, his costly raiments will
offer him no delight. What matters it, on the
other hand, if his possessions are small, if his
home is plain, if his clothes are simple; if he
is contented with them all, he is a rich and a
happy man. For the contented man is never

poor, the discontented never rich. If we fasten
our attention on what we have, rather than on
what we lack, we shall find that a very little is
enough to satisfy us. Contented folk are im-
mune from misfortune, they are free from
worry, from fear, from anxiety; for the real
needs of man are far less than what they are
deemed to be. The basic needs of food and
clothing and shelter are easily supplied; it is
the desire for a great surplus above these needs
that breeds discontent in the human heart.
But the good that contentment brings with it
far surpasses any other wealth that man may
attain. Contentment destroys chagrin, it softens disappointment; it brings forth the finer
elements of the human soul; it keeps man
serene, his mind poised and calm, his heart
warm and sympathetic. Discontent, on the
other hand, nurtures naught but poisonous,
pernicious influences.

If we teach the doctrine of contentment, if
we urge that man find satisfaction in what he
has, what, you may inquire, will prompt him to
greater achievement, to more intensive growth?
We have, as before indicated, drawn a line of
demarcation between two kinds of discontent:

discontent with possessions, and discontent
with attainment; discontent with what one has
and discontent with what one is. Let one be
always contented with what he has, for here
discontent leads only to unhappiness; but let
one never be content with what he is, for here
contentment leads only to stagnation. To have
enough is one thing, but to do enough, to know
enough, to think enough, to feel enough, to
achieve enough, to be great enough, to be good
enough, is quite another matter. Never say to
yourself: "I am wise enough, I need no more
knowledge." Seek rather constantly to increase the fund of your knowledge, seek always
to add to the repository of your wisdom. No
matter how much you know, there is always
more to learn. There is no limitation, no end
to mental growth. Be not contented with yourself. Do not say to yourself: "I have achieved
enough." You have not. You may have
achieved enough for yourself, you may have
amassed enough, but you have not achieved
enough. The world is waiting for your *disin-
terested,* unselfish achievements; mankind is
waiting for you to lend it your efforts, your
experience, your wealth, to make it better and

happier. Do not be contented with yourself. Do not say, "I am good enough, or kind enough or charitable enough." For the moment you make such a claim you stunt the growth of your own heart, you dwarf your own spirit, you put a stoppage to your unfoldment. Do not be contented with yourself. Aspire always to higher conquests of yourself, reach out always for the realization of greater ideals, expand the depths of your soul, and you shall find an ever-increasing happiness in life.

One who is discontented with what he has and discontented with what he is, may achieve great things; he may build and create and acquire, but he will never find happiness; something will always haunt him, always gnaw at the roots of his heart, always pursue him; he will never find himself. One who is contented with what he has and with what he is, will experience quietude and peace, but he will achieve nothing, accomplish nothing, create nothing in life. He will be contented, but will always remain at the same height. It is only the one who is contented with what he has, and discontented with what he is, who will build and achieve and also know peace and happiness.

HOW TO BEGIN THE DAY

"Be careful of the beginning of your task," said a sage of olden times, "for the beginning will give the tone to the whole." We add here, be watchful also of the beginning of your *day*, for the keynote of the day is sounded at its beginning. Begin the day aright, and the day will be a source of blessing unto you. Begin the day with caution and it will be a successful one. Begin the day judiciously and it will yield you an abundant measure of happiness. The character and rhythm of a symphony are determined by its first movement; the glory of the day is determined by its first ray of light; the success and happiness of a man's day are determined by his first step— his first step in the morning becomes the model for the subsequent steps of the day. Man's mood in the morning becomes the keynote to his mood for the day; his morning's temper becomes his day's temper; his pessimism in the early hours only spreads and deepens with the succeeding hours; likewise, his enthusiasm and optimism of the morning grow in strength and in depth during the day. It is therefore of exceeding importance to direct with care and with watchfulness the initial step of our day.

First of all, it is vital that we begin the day without haste. One must begin the day even as God Himself begins it. The day does not begin with a sudden rush of life; there is no sudden intensity of daylight; there is no instant replacement of the night's atmosphere; there is no impulsive and sudden awakening of the dormant forces of nature; and the moon and the stars do not recede hastily or disappear in one swooping moment. God does not perform His tasks in haste, nature does not hurry. Man, who is a child of God, must follow the method of God in his own work; man, who is an integral part of nature, must follow the method of nature in his own achievements; the method of the great universal processes of creation must be reflected in man's processes of creation. We therefore re-iterate: Do not begin the day with a rush. To rush in the morning is an unnatural way and therefore a ruinous way of beginning. If you rush in the morning, you will necessarily continue to rush during the day. In the morning, you prepare your nervous system for the day; in the morning you set its pace for the day; in the morning you unconsciously give it its rhythm for the day, and all the reactions of the day will trace their origin to the first reaction, to the initial mood. If you begin the day in haste, you will rush throughout the day, even if there is nothing to be rushing for; you will be filled with excitement, even if the rest of the world is serene; you will be rushing about even if your tasks do not require it and your duties are light. For your nerves have unconsciously, inaudibly, been told to go fast, and they simply carry out your instructions; they go fast, they carry you fast throughout the day.

Begin the day, therefore, with poise and serenity. Begin the day in the natural way and you will be well rewarded. Retire not at a late hour, and you will be able to rise at an early hour, and then the hands of the clock will not need to urge you, they will not drive you, nor warn you, nor threaten you. They will tell you instead: "There is plenty of time." Begin the day with the tranquility which an early rising induces, and the rest of the day will be serene.

You will then achieve your tasks with ease, you will do your work in peace, you will not wait impatiently for the last hour of your work to draw nigh, and you will take delight in every task, in every hour of the day. Begin the day in serenity, and your faculties will do their work faithfully, your mind will dig its deepest channels, your judgment will show the clearest ways, your imagination will take its highest flights; your ambition, your aspiration, will manifest their most concentrated, dynamic powers.

Begin the day with serenity, and in addition, begin the day with a cheerful heart, begin the day with a smile. The night is not only a period of rest, it is also a period of forgetfulness, it is also a great deep in which man drowns the unpleasant experiences of the day. In the morning therefore be sure that you do not draw up the discarded heaviness of the day before. Do not recall and recount the mishaps of the day gone by. Do not begin the day with anxiety over the past. Anxiety is the rust of life, destroying its lustre and weakening its power. Yesterday is here no more; its atmosphere has vanished, its clouds dissolved, its hours obliterated, why then foster its troubles; why keep alive its unhappiness? Why not let these, too, follow into oblivion the day in which they were born? So do not begin the day with the heavy burdens of yesterday. Nor do you begin the day with anticipation of difficulty and trouble for to-day. Remember how much health, how much strength, how much vitality have cost us the evils that have never happened. How much strain, how much anxiety, how much fear have cost us forebodings that have never been justified. Therefore cast aside these forebodings and fruitless anxieties and begin the day with a cheerful heart and smiling eyes. And how much easier will be the burden of the difficulties that actually confront us if we meet them with a smiling front. Therefore we say again begin the day with a smile, begin the day with a joyful heart, even as the day itself opens with a smile, even as the creatures of nature open the day with joyous song, even as children open the day with laughter and glee. And if you smile in the early part of the day, your joy will be continuous throughout the day. You will then meet every exigency, every obstacle with unbattered cheer; then your burdens will not oppress you, their weight will not bear you down, you will meet their challenge without discouragement and without hurt. Your smile, kindled in the early morning, will carry you safe and sound throughout the day. What did God create in the beginning? In the beginning he created sunshine, and because of it the rest of creation was possible and easy. Begin your day with sunshine and the achievements of your day will be easy and pleasant.

Begin your day with serenity and with cheer, but also with love and good-will towards the whole world. Begin the day with an open mind and an open heart. Do not begin with the feeling that you are one entity and the world another and distinct one. Do not begin with the thought that you and the rest of mankind are two,—two distinct centres of life and interests. This is not so. You and the world are one, you and the rest of mankind are inherently one. There is the same flow of life in all men, there is the same vibration in all minds, there is the same pulse in all hearts, there is the same divinity in action in all of us and through all of us. We are only different ripples of the same ocean, we are only different shades of the same colorful horizon, we are only different rays of the same overwhelming Fountain of Light. Because we are one, we must feel as one. We must not begin the day with the bitterness that divides the hearts of men; we must not begin the day with a grudge that drives a wedge between us and a fellow-man; we must not begin the day with the intention of making someone hot, or furious or unhappy; we must not begin the day with a purpose that will mortify a fellow-man or beat him to the ground. Begin the day with love, with good-will for everyone. Let the natural unity, the natural harmony between man and man assert itself; do not obstruct its way, let it find expression through you. Begin the day with good-will and sympathy and you will draw unto yourself the good-will and sympathy of the rest of your kind. The world will treat you just as you treat the world; mankind will repay you with the substance that you offer it. The world will give sympathy for sympathy and love for love.

Begin your day with serenity, with joy and with good-will. Begin also your day with prayer. Give the first ten minutes of your wakefulness to prayer. God's help should be invoked in every task and in every enterprise; he should be asked to direct our every thought, to guide our every feeling. God is the source of our life, He is our Sustainer and Protector; therefore in our prayer we simply declare our happiness in His Presence and seek His guidance and help. We experience true safety, true joy, only by first seeking God, and through prayer we experience God's presence and God's help. Prayer is the language in which man speaks to God, it is the channel through which the human mind communicates with the Divine Mind. The more you communicate with Him, the more you come to know Him, the more you understand His ways, the more do you receive His blessing.

Be watchful of the beginning, and you are taking care of the whole. Begin the day, be-gin *each* day with serenity, with joy, with good-will, with prayer, and you assure yourself a perfect life. You cannot dream of a serene old age, unless you now begin each day with serenity; you cannot dream of a joyful future, unless you begin each day joyfully; you cannot speak of universal peace and love, unless you begin each day with love and good-will to everyone; you cannot speak of God's ways and God's help, unless you seek Him each day of your life, unless you open each one of your days with prayer.

THE SPRING OF LIFE

Every season of the year is rich in beauty and in splendor. Each of them is a divine masterpiece. Each one speaks of eternal majesty, each one reveals endless glories stored away at the very beginning of creation. But although each one manifests grandeur and glory, yet the one that stirs us most, that animates us most, that brings us most delight, is the season of spring.

Spring is the season of creation. The fields and the mountains clothe themselves in green, the flowers break through the earth and project themselves into the life-giving sunshine, the trees breathe with freshness and warmth, yielding again the signals of life and growth. Even the steadfast stars appear brighter, the sun's smiles happier, the whole universe alive with new power and new hope.

Because it is a season of creation, spring is also a season of revelation; for God is revealed through his works. The earth has no mind of itself, the sprouts and the blossoms have no consciousness of their own, the clouds and the stars do not plan their own courses, the streams and the winds have no guidance of themselves, and yet they all act with wisdom, they all follow their courses with understanding, they work together with harmony and co-operation. If they do not direct themselves, do we not see that a Universal Mind, an all-encompassing Mind, a Divine Mind, expresses Himself through them, sustaining them and directing them, supplying them with substance and energy, and implanting harmony within them so that they all work in unison. Do we not behold God revealing Himself in nature, working through nature, manifesting His power and His wisdom through every form, through every being, through every essence of existence?

The season of spring has its message to man in all stages of his life. It speaks its message to youth. Spring has been termed the youth of the year, and youth is aptly to be regarded as the spring of life. In youth, in the spring of life, the sun is brightest, the sky is clearest, the horizon vast and infinite. Love and affection speak in the heart within, and in nature without; song, mirth, sprightliness, hopefulness, all commingle to make life pleasant and sweet. In the spring of life, there are no clouds, there is no sadness. Optimism overpowers everything, hope occupies the foremost place in the mind. In the spring of life, the gates of the world are just opening; every experience is keenly felt, every new sight is deeply enjoyed, every unfamiliar region, every unknown countenance, excites curiosity and desire for knowledge and exploration. In the spring of life, the senses work with overwhelming power, the heart beats with vigor, the limbs move with ease, free from all burdens. At that period, impressions engrave themselves most deeply upon the mind, the procession of experiences leave their indelible negatives upon the plastic memory, emotions flow from the heart with impetuosity and without restraint. This is youth, this is the spring of life.

But the message of spring to youth is *growth*. Youth, because of its impressionable nature, because of its flexibility and mouldability, must constantly aim at growth. Man can always acquire knowledge, he should always strive to acquire wisdom. But the knowledge and the wisdom that one attains in youth, are the acquisitions which count most in life. Early knowledge, early wisdom, illumine one's path, they equip the individual with clearer vision, they lend more stability, more certainty, more self-assurance, in the quest for a goal. Early knowledge makes one's way in life easier, it gives one a more correct evaluation of life and things, it leads him more directly to his life purpose.

And just as youth is an especially advantageous period for the growth of the mind, so is it also the most favorable period for the growth of character. It is never too late to enrich the heart, or direct the emotions into noble expression; but of all periods in man's life, youth is the most propitious for this end. When the growth of character is undertaken in youth, the task is an easier one. For then there is little to uproot, little to destroy; the best conquers almost without resistance, nobility gains its victory with little struggle. When character is planted in youth, its fruit is sound, it carries with it a fragrance of genuine sweetness that delights the heart.

The message of spring to youth is none other, then, than that of growth; for "youth is the text of life, while the other periods are only interpretations," and it is the clearness of the text that determines the nature of the interpretations. Youth is the fountain-head of life, and the subsequent periods are but the streams flowing from it; the clearness of the stream is greatly determined by the purity of its fount. Youth, it has been said, is the spring of life, and it therefore determines the luxuriance of the summer, the abundance of the autumn, and the provisions for the winter.

But spring has a message to man in all stages of his life, to his maturity as well as to his youth. Now what is the message that spring brings to maturity? The bright days of spring always come after a period of dreariness and cold; the sun of spring always shines after much cloudiness and gloom; the freedom of spring bursts forth after much confinement and incarceration. Spring has a message of optimism, and it is brought to man even after his early period of mirth has passed. A man may find himself beset by difficulties, he may be confronted with obstacles and perplexities, he may even be facing suffering; but let him not lose hope, let him not lose faith, let him not lose courage, let him not permit the heaviness of his burdens to weigh down upon his spirit, to dishearten him from his purpose, to submerge him in despondency. Let him only firmly remember that after winter spring must come, that brighter days are ahead, that it is the law of God that dreariness and misery and coldness must vanish and give way to sunshine and brightness and warmth.

The more one refuses to identify himself with the gloomy and the pessimistic phases of life, and the more he directs his gaze to the hopeful and the optimistic horizon, the more does he hasten the arrival of the brighter days. Each man is his own Messiah, and the more he craves and seeks self-deliverance the sooner does his redemption come. A man may sustain financial losses, but these will not hurt him if together with these he does not lose his courage. He may lose even his entire fortune, and yet if he retains his hope and his spirit, he will emerge uninjured. For with courage and with hope, with spirit and with faith, he can set himself to the task of clearing the ruins, lay a new foundation and build a new structure—a structure even larger than the one that was demolished. To build is the sole purpose of a man's life. To build, not necessarily to amass, is the chief aim of existence. So does it matter much, in building, whether we are adding greater heights to the top, or rising again from the bottom to the top? In each case, our interest in life is stirred and deepened, our mind wide-awake, our spirit re-awakened, our aspiration, our whole being kept in action. So when we find ourselves knocked down by circumstances, and despair begins to make its way into our consciousness, let us always carry in our mind a vision of brighter days and happier times, of more sunshine and clearer atmosphere, which will unfailingly come. Dreariness is not here forever, spring is coming towards us.

Spring holds out a message also to those who have attained old age, to those who are losing interest in this life and are centering their vision on the hereafter, who are standing before the gates of mystery, attempting to peer through the veil. To these, spring speaks clearly of hope and of life to come. The grass, the flowers, that come to life in the spring, have once been buried under the heavy crust of the

earth. But with the spring they become recharged with life and with strength; they rise
again to join the chorus of creation and take
their place in adding harmony and riches to
the universe. For this is the plan of God:
that nothing shall be destroyed, but that all
things shall grow and flourish again; there
is an inherent immortality in things created by
God. If it is God's wish that the mute flower
should not vanish forever, if it is His design
that even the insignificant blade of grass shall
not be annihilated, how much clearer, how
much more potent does our belief in man's immortality become. We are not born to be wiped
out of existence, we are born to grow; we grow
in this world, and when our growth on this
earth has become complete, we grow from this
world into another world. Death therefore has
no terror for us, the fear of annihilation has
vanished. Death only marks a new destina-
tion, a new height from which greater beauties
may be beheld, greater glories discerned and
greater happiness attained.

Spring is thus the open volume in which we
may read the true history of human existence.
In it are prescribed our functions, in it are

models furnished for our moods, and in it also the ultimate destiny of our existence is revealed. Let us read the book of spring with understanding, and our life will be illumined by its message.

THE POWER OF WORDS

What is it that represents most faithfully the inner life of man to the outer world? It is not his appearance, for this, as we know, is frequently misleading and deceiving. A man may appear vigorous, strong, yet in reality, may be the victim of illness and suffering; on the other hand, one may appear frail, and yet possess great resources of energy and power. One may appear timid, and yet be charged with great courage, or one may appear severe, even fierce, and yet be of a mild, tender disposition. We therefore say that a man's appearance is not the most faithful representation of the man. Nor do a man's manners always represent him correctly, for while manners often express the qualities of one's inner being, they do not constitute the best standard by which an individual may be tested and judged; for manners are not inherent in man, but are acquired by man; they are pleasing habits obtained through observation and training; and it is a common experience to come upon men of uncouth man-

ners but of sterling character, and vice-versa,
of excellent manners but of rude disposition.
We therefore say that manners too are not the
most faithful indicators of the souls of men.

Man, we believe, is most clearly exposed by
his words. What a man says, how he says it,
the meaning behind each word, the gesture that
accompanies each utterance, the softness or the
harshness in each tone, the mirth or the sullen-
ness, the attentiveness or the indifference, that
are impregnated in the words, they all portray
the man. The qualities of a man's mind, the
depth of his thoughts, the magnitude of his
vision, the nature of his interests and aspirations are all expressed in his words. Likewise
are the qualities of character frequently made
manifest in one's speech. Although we say, in
matters of conduct, that deeds speak louder
than words, yet man's utterances concerning
character are usually the keynote to his ideals,
they point the direction in which he aspires to
go. For it is seldom that one lauds that to
which he is inwardly indifferent, or praises that
which he silently considers without merit, or
seeks to be identified with that which he does
not believe beneficial and sound. Man's speech

also displays man's temperament, his moods, his disposition. For there is one personality behind hasty words and another behind deliberate words; cheerful words emanate from a cheerful disposition, sour and embittered utterances indicate an opposite mood and temperament. Words, it is clear, represent man most vividly and accurately to his fellow-man.

But while we say that speech or words are the most faithful ambassadors of man's personality, yet the function of speech is greater than that of furnishing colors for the delineation of man's inner life. The purpose of words is fundamentally to place man in communication with his fellow-man. It is language that unites man with man; it is language that furnishes the link between soul and soul, it is language that makes it possible for men to live in groups and to unite in enterprise for the common good.

It is especially when we reflect upon language as the medium of contact and communication among men that we are able to realize the power of words. There are kind words and there are mean words, there are words which animate, which encourage and stimulate and there are words which wound and hurt, which terrify and humiliate. There are words which are like a healing balm, which soothe and cheer, and banish misery and stifle despondency; and there are words which oppress the heart and cause anguish and anxiety and make the burdens of life heavier. There are words which bring out the best in us, inspire us to greater efforts, urge us on to higher achievements, lift us from low to high levels; and there are words which retard our progress, discourage our efforts and keep our faculties imprisoned and silent. Words, in so far as they affect and influence the lives of others, are the most vital and most powerful factors in human life.

It is in this light that we are able to appreciate the admonitions of prophets and sages against an evil tongue, and also, on the other hand, the rewards they promised for kindly words. One of the greatest attainments in human life is to train one's tongue in such a fashion that it should always yield pleasant words. Bridle it, therefore, with all your power, restrain it with all your might, direct it with the best that is in you, that from it may issue forth only your kindest and your finest.

Speak kindly. Speak kindly to people and speak kindly of people. Speak kindly to people; a kind word leaves a most lasting and powerful impression. A kind word is not flattery, it is not false adulation, it is not conventional compliment. A kind word has this characteristic about it: it always encourages; it encourages to greater achievements, it encourages to cleaner and finer conduct, it leads to greater happiness. A kind word kindles hope in despondent eyes, and lifts a downcast spirit; a kind word will make a reticent tongue speak, and stir silent thoughts into action. A kind word assuages anger, creates friendship in the hearts of enemies, turns bitterness into good-will and transmutes hatred into sympathy and love. A kind word is the true expression of humaneness, for humaneness can only be understood in terms of kindness, it can only be effective when it is embodied in the quality of kindness. A kind word represents the wisdom of all the ages; it represents the preachings of the prophets, the ethical teachings of the sages, the fruits of all the minds that strove and sacrificed for the advancement of humanity.

And just as one ought to speak kindly to people, so ought he also to speak kindly of people. One cannot truly speak kindly to people unless he also speaks kindly of people. Speaking kindly to people means encouragement, speaking kindly of people entails appreciation and respect. One can encourage people only when he respects them and appreciates them. The cynic or the scoffer, who always finds people uncouth or disharmonious or ludicrous, has never cherished any respect for them and never been able to speak kindly to them. The fault seeker and the fault finder have never been able to encourage and to help people. The critical and the narrow-hearted have never been able to strengthen and help others. It is only those who appreciate human beings, who respect them and honor them, that are able to give them help and strength.

To speak kindly of people one must be imbued with a certain sense of generosity. For just as there are men who look upon money given to charity as a grievous detraction from their own fortune, failing to understand that charity is the greatest of spiritual investments, so are there those who regard words of praise in behalf of others as entailing depreciation of their own selves; they feel that by praising and admiring others they are indicating that their own qualities are inferior, else why admire them; they are instead inclined to slander others under the delusion that this would establish them as free from the faults they deplore. In speaking of others, one must overcome these petty, vain, unbecoming inclinations, and show large-heartedness in their stead. One must see and express the fineness, the goodness, the greatness in others. And in being generous with one's words, as with one's purse, no loss is involved, for generosity is a purifier of the spirit and wins to itself friends and enemies alike.

We have said before that man's personality is expressed in his words; but it is true also that man may be moulded by his words. For just as man makes words, so may words make man. Words, whether expressed by others or by oneself, create mental images, generate thought processes, and actually create tendencies and dispositions. As for example, when kind words are spoken they usually emanate from the heart, but if they do not emanate from the heart and there is still an intention of

kindness behind them, these words nevertheless impress themselves strongly upon the heart
of the one who has uttered them and there
they create around themselves sets of emotions
which harmonize with the content of kindliness
which they expressed.   Words not only dig
impressions into the material before them, but
they also leave traces behind them.   And it is
for this reason that kindly words, if they were
not felt before they were uttered, are felt after
they have been spoken, and turn the heart in
the same direction.

THE POWER OF AN IDEAL

As we study the history of races and nations, we become impressed by this one outstanding truth, that whenever a nation identified itself with an ideal and toiled and struggled for its promotion, it always met with success. It became irresistible in battle, it fought against superior numbers and emerged victorious, it manifested gigantic strength and heroism. It stood out among other nations like a high tower, like a blazing star in a dim sky. Its destiny was so bright that it appeared to be specially favored by God. Look upon the glorious history of small Greece, look upon the still more glorious history of Israel in Zion, and you will behold the power of a people imbued with an ideal. Small as these nations were in the days of antiquity, yet their spirit shed an influence over the whole of mankind, which continues still to this day.

We find, on the other hand, that a people who had no spiritual goal, or who abandoned their spiritual goal, no longer identifying themselves with a national ideal, were often, despite vast numbers, highly vulnerable, wanting in courage and endurance, in unity and in enthusiasm, and subject to attack and disintegration.

There is a great measure of similarity between the life of an individual, and the life of a multitude. The soul of the individual contains the same essence, the same ingredients, as does the soul of a nation. The individual, too, lives his best when he lives his highest, he lives his happiest when he lives his greatest, he too is invincible when he identifies his life with an ideal. An ideal gives meaning to one's life, it adds purpose to one's existence, it brings forth the best that is in one's soul, it draws out the finest, the noblest that is in one's heart, it elevates one to a plane of beauty and harmony and happiness.

Let us pause for a moment here to give a definition of our subject. What is an ideal? An ideal is a mental image of the most noble and therefore the most desirable state in which one would wish either himself or society to be. Such an image is created by the best in man. Man carries a noble model in his imagination either of what he himself should be, or of what human society, in which he lives, should be. The deep, spiritual forces in man unite to show him the way to a higher life and they paint a picture of perfection in his imagination; and this mental picture man calls an ideal: a picture of things not as they are, but as they should be; it deals not with what man has already acquired, but with what man should pursue and even struggle to attain. An ideal is therefore a picture of a larger life, and there is, as a rule, a vast distance between man's life as it is and the life he idealizes for himself.

Man's greatness, however, does not lie in his possession of an ideal; every one may have a lofty ideal; it lies in his efforts to realize the ideal. Ideals themselves are but ethereal models; as far as we know they have no existence in this tangible world. But they can be made real, they can take on shape and form through human effort. The distance between man's actual state and the ideal can be conquered, the gulf can be bridged, man can reach his ideal and clothe his spirit with it.

I said that an ideal may be a vision either of a higher self or of a nobler environment. A man must carry in his imagination, no matter how high a state of being he has attained, an image of himself ever greater than the actual state in which he is, a state which he still must struggle to attain. Men who have been great never saw themselves as perfect, they never saw themselves through the eyes of their admirers, but, on the contrary, no matter what height they had climbed to, always saw a greater self before them which they must still struggle to realize. There is no state of completion in one's development, one must keep ever growing, and one's ideal too must ever grow.

Together with his task, together with his business and daily duties, man must always foster an ideal, something which is above material attainment, something that has nothing to do with possession or with wealth. A man may be wealthy, possess great treasures, and yet be a small man. Or one may be poor, even destitute, and have about him the aura of greatness. For greatness and smallness have nought to do with gross treasures, they have to do with man himself, they have to do with man's ideals of life and of himself.

An ideal, I have said, implies improvement. An ideal may be either an improvement of the mind or an improvement of the heart, or of both. The mind must always be stimulated to growth. Psychology shows us that man uses but a small part of his brain; there are layers of thought-producing energy which are not used at all. Man is therefore capable of greater wisdom, of more knowledge, of a deeper grasp of things than he usually has. We live in a limitless world; there is so much to be known, so much to understand, so much to think about, so much to study and comprehend. A man cannot possibly, during his life career, take in everything into the realm of his thought, but he can, assuredly, embrace a great deal of a great many things. He need not leave it entirely to the philosopher to rationalize for him, or to the psychologist to observe for him, or to the physical scientist to analyze for him, or to the historian to reconstruct the past for him. Man is capable of being his own philosopher, his own psychologist, even his own scientist and his own theologian. He must utilize the study, the experience, the acumen of the experts in the various fields of knowledge; but he must not neglect his own search for knowledge because there are those who know, or his own thinking because there are those who think. Just as one endeavors to accumulate a measure of wealth for himself, so also must he collect a fund of knowledge of his own. Aside from its utilitarian aspect, there is a thrill in knowledge. Men often spend fortunes in order to break the monotony in their lives, in order to be thrilled by new experiences. I say that there are thrills in knowledge. There are thrills in learning of the treasures of the sea, there are thrills in studying the wonders of the earth, there are thrills in clearing the mysteries of the remote sky. There are thrills in finding how the bird builds its nest, how it feeds and shelters and protects its young; there are thrills in discovering how the beast digs its den, and hunts its food, and guards itself against invading foes; there are thrills in the history of past generations, in the struggle of those who lived before us, who attained, who achieved for posterity; there are thrills in studying even the ways of the insignificant worm. There are thrills in the knowledge of every law, every process, every being, in God's creation. You can see therefore that the ideal of knowledge has even immediate rewards; it opens the portals to a larger world, it makes life deep, rich and interesting.

And just as an ideal can center itself on the improvement of the mind, so can it also take for its aim the improvement of the heart. The heart, like the mind, has far greater capabilities than we imagine it to possess. Our feelings are much deeper, our emotions are much keener, more tender than those we give expression to. God endowed man with emotions in order to establish a firm relationship between himself and his fellow man. A world without sympathy, without love, without compassion, would be but a desiccated world. There is no word mightier and more expressive in human language than the word "goodness." Thought, we are told, rules the world, but it is goodness that holds it together. Thought without goodness would still continue to make the world progress in certain directions, but it would be a cold and dreary world, nevertheless. Without the emotions of goodness, men would always be strangers to one another, they would keep themselves within the confines of their own shadows, they would be capable of knowing only their own needs, of realizing only their own wishes and desires. And although this may actually be the case with certain individuals, we know at least that it is not an expression of their natural self, that somewhere deep in their consciousness there is something fine and noble which can be appealed to. If man were without emotion, without goodness, nothing in him would respond even to the tenderest appeal. Without goodness, without tenderness, without a willingness to be helpful to one another, there could be no co-operation, there could be no union, no organized society, not even a true family life, for all these find their basis in goodness, in tenderness, and in love.

Because man is divinely endowed with goodness, he can make goodness his ideal. To help one who solicits your help is noble, but it is not the only way in which the ideal acts. One who makes goodness his ideal goes out in search for opportunities to do good. He makes efforts to console the sorrowful, to cheer the depressed, to give hope to the despondent, to help those who are in need and in want. Those whose ideal is goodness identify themselves with institutions the aim of which is to show mankind the better, the nobler way of living, and dedicate themselves, their efforts, their whole soul to the promotion of these agencies of human goodness.   Those whose ideal is goodness seek to generate love and good will among men, and promote peace in the world.

I said that there was a thrill in knowledge, but let me say that there is an even greater thrill in the performance of good acts.   When our deeper emotions have the opportunity for free expression, they leave behind them a trail of happiness.   No man engaged in the noble task of helping others has ever felt unhappy himself, no man engaged in encouraging, in cheering others has ever failed to receive cheer and courage himself.   No man, striving and working for the promotion of a beneficent institution, has ever failed to receive spiritual benefits himself.   There is indeed a thrill and a throb of joy in the expression of goodness.

One must have an ideal, and it must entail the improvement of the mind or of the heart, or of both.   No man is alone who fosters an ideal, the ideal is his animating companion.   No man can be small whose heart is the home of a great ideal. The ideal will make his whole being great, it will bring out the deepest and the highest in him. No man who cherishes an ideal can find life empty or dull or monotonous or devoid of purpose. No man can fail to find true happiness who gives himself to an ideal.

MAN—MASTER OR SERVANT?

What is the destiny of man?   Answers the apostle of pessimism: Man is an insignificant creature in an ınfinite world, a leaf caught in the fury of the elements, a servant of the soil, a slave of his own desires. Answers the Psalmist: "Thou hast made him but little lower than the angels, Thou hast crowned him with glory and honor, Thou hast made him to have dominion over the works of Thy hands, Thou hast put all things under his feet."

Considering these two opposite views of the destiny of man, we ask ourselves which of these two may we regard as true?   What is man, servant or master?   Is it our destiny to dominate, to mould things in accordance with our will, to rise and tower above the environment and be master of all that is about us? Or are we born slaves?   Is it man's nature to subordinate himself to his environment, to resign himself to every unfavorable circumstance, to submit to every influence that seeks to gain mastery over him?   Which of the two disposi-

tions are inherent in man, servitude, or the will
to rule?

If we weigh this question accurately, and
carefully analyze man's nature, we find that
man was originally endowed with both. He has
within him powers that make for mastery, and
also characteristics that enable him to give himself as a servant.

Let us be clear, before we proceed, as to
the true distinction between servant and master,
for these two terms have been miscellaneously
applied and variously used. By master we
mean one who follows the direction of his own
will; by servant we mean one who follows the
will of some one else. The master follows the
dictates of his own will even though the wills
of others are not in harmony with his, even
though he meets opposition and resistance. The
servant, on the other hand, follows the will
of another, even though this may involve the
crushing and immolation of his own will.

He who is master may exercise his will in
various directions. He may extend his will over
other human beings, ruling them and directing
them. He may also exercise his will over circumstances, moulding and fashioning them in

accordance with his ambitions or in harmony with his tastes. Conversely, the servant may submit his will to the will of another man, becoming his tool or his messenger; or he may surrender his will to the will of the masses; he may become servant to the group, its tool and its messenger.

Man being born with capacities for both mastery and servitude, the question arises as to how are these diametrically opposite powers to be employed by the same individual; when is one to be master and when is he to be servant? Is such a condition at all possible? We say it is. We say, in Jewish Science, that while man may debase himself in the wrongful use of these opposite tendencies within him, yet is it within his reach, through the use of these same tendencies, to attain the highest degree of self-expression. There are two outstanding spheres, in one of which man must be master, and in the other of which he must seek to act as a servant. Man must be absolute master over himself, and he must strive to be the servant of mankind.

Man must aim to become master of himself. What does this involve? Man's inner world does not at all resemble the outer world in which he finds himself. In the world outside of man, there is order. Every star knows its orbit, every wind knows its course, every sprout knows its season, every stream knows its confines and its goal. In the world outside of man, there is also harmony; not only does each phenomenon in nature know its own law and its own course, not only does it undeviatingly perform its duty in its own sphere, but it also acts so as to co-operate with the other phenomena, with the other forces in nature, so that they too can follow their laid-out path. In the world outside of man there is also unity; that is, all forces, all influences in nature work towards one common goal, they all act and work for the advancement and enhancement of the world. Every star adds more light to the world, every flower adds more beauty to the world, every tree more strength, every stream more delight, more animation to the world,—they all work for one common goal, the enrichment of the world.

But in the world within man, there is not this undeviating order, there is not this perfect harmony; nor do we find there this highly concentrated purposive unity. If we could look into the invisible world within man, we would be amazed at the incongruity, the disharmony existing within. Thoughts of the most contradictory nature sojourn together, feelings of the most conflicting kind reside side by side; the most heterogeneous desires, the most discordant wishes, the most dissimilar ambitions dwell within the limited circumference of the same mind. Here is an inner world of confusion as against an outer world of perfect order. There is order and harmony and unity in the world outside of man, because there is a Master that controls and directs everything; there is chaos and confusion in the mind of man, in his inner world, because he has not learned to direct and control the various elements therein.

To be master over one's inner world, to be master over oneself, means, first, to be master over the realm of one's thoughts,—to allow expansion for those thoughts which are pertinent and serviceable, and not to allow oneself to be carried away into the realm of dreams and fancies at the expense of vital, practical thought. The human mind is not a very diligent instrument, it has no voluntary liking for things involving effort and constraint, it likes to fly in free, aimless motion. The master must therefore direct the mind-energy and force it into channels by which it will bring the highest usefulness and the greatest results. The master, likewise, must not allow the mind to take a downward swoop; pessimism and moroseness of any kind, in which the human mind frequently likes to indulge, must be checked at once and annihilated. I do not mean to say that one should render himself insensible to danger, that he should close his eyes, overlook pitfalls and say to himself that they do not exist. A man should indeed be wide-awake, but he should forbid his mind to be overcome by peril, and should, on the contrary, urge it to work and find the way out of apparent difficulty. The master of his mind need not be possessed of a master-mind, but he must force his mental powers to produce their best and their most useful thoughts, meet obstacles with courage and resourcefulness and not permit himself to be dragged down into pessimism or despair.

Just as one must strive to be master over his thoughts, so must he also seek to be master

over his emotions.   There are a multitude of
wholesome feelings in man's breast, but there
are also emotions, impulses, impetuosities
which should be checked and exterminated.
There is emotional energy which expresses itself in the form of anger, or bitterness, or revenge.   There are words uttered in moments of
impulse which bring nothing but regret; there
are acts perpetrated in moments of rage which
in his lucid hours man would give much to re-
trieve and wipe out from his memory.   The
master first *chooses* his emotions and then de-
livers himself to them.   He first realizes which
of his feelings are wholesome and beneficial
and then identifies himself with them.   And just
as he gives expression to his wholesome emotions, so does he check and suppress those impulses in his nature which serve only ignoble
ends.

We emphasize self-mastery in Jewish Science,
because we believe that when one succeeds in
gaining dominion over his mind and over his
emotions, he is a true master and he is ful-
filling the divine intention with which the powers of mastery were given him.

In the same degree in which man seeks to

become master of himself, so must he also seek to become servant to mankind. There may not be much joy in being a servant to an individual, but there is the greatest joy in becoming a servant to the multitude. To become a servant of mankind means to devote oneself to the task of making the life of others easier and happier. The human order in which we are living is not at all perfect. There is a great deal of unhappiness among men. There is a great deal of suffering, a great deal of want, a great deal of injustice, a great deal of disappointment, a great deal of sorrow. The reason for this lies in the fact that men do not know how to live. The true servant of mankind is the devoted woman and the earnest man who seek to eliminate some of the misery in the world, to ameliorate some of the evil conditions, to banish at least some of its suffering, to make the burdens of at least some souls lighter to bear, to brighten at least some faces, to kindle hope in some human hearts. These are the true servants of the people.

This servitude is a *higher* state in human development than self-mastery. One must first master himself before he becomes capable of serving others. One must first master his selfishness before he can give himself wholeheartedly to others; one must first subdue his self-centeredness before he willingly gives his strength to the service of others; one must first banish his own pessimism before he is able to drive out pessimism in others. One must first become master of himself before he can attain the higher level of becoming the servant of mankind.

The great immortal souls that have lived among us were servants of the people. The prophets who sought to illumine the paths of men were servants of the people. The psalmists and seers who burningly sought to implant faith in a Benevolent Father were servants of the people. The men and women of all times who willingly offered themselves, even to their lives, sacrificing their own desires, surrendering their own comforts, to better the condition of others, were servants of the people.

Each one is divinely endowed with these two sets of gifts. Each one has the powers that make for mastery and the characteristics that make for servanthood; each one can use these gifts divinely and be master of himself, servant of mankind.

THE TYRANNY OF THE PAST

As we look into the depths of our being, we find our personality composed of divers tendencies, many of which are wholesome and elevating and conducive to happiness, others of which, on the other hand, are injurious to our being, impediments to our spirit, and destructive to our happiness. We can easily trace the source of the good that is within us, for we know that we are created in the divine image, and are therefore possessed of attributes reflecting divinity; but to what origin can we ascribe the noxious elements in our disposition? We know, indeed, that they are present, for we are both the implements for and the victims of their expression, but how did these disturbing factors gain entrance at all into our being? The nearest answer we can give to this is that we are greatly products of the past, that we are the embodiments of proclivities and reactions, generated and transmitted to us by the past, that we are sprouts whose stems have been planted in the past.

Now what are the deleterious reactions in our nature for the presence of which we charge the past? They are indeed too numerous for mention, but we may center, at this moment, on a few which are more universal and common.

A man displays his weakness, first of all, when he expresses anger. When in anger, man does not deliberate; he is, in fact, incapable of reasoning; he is incapable of good judgment and clear understanding; his vision is blurred, his rational faculties are silent, his humanity paralyzed. In his moment of anger man violates all the standards of mankind; he is neither gentle nor just nor reasonable; all the landmarks of civilization are at that moment wiped out, all the checks of refinement and convention are dissolved, all the restraints imposed by wisdom are severed. In his wrath, man also transgresses the laws of God. Love, sympathy, forgiveness, righteousness, are all violently cast out of his consciousness. At that moment, he becomes a destructive being—a being which he would despise and condemn in others, when his serener self holds sway. A man in his rage becomes indeed a repugnant likeness of himself

—a picture which he himself repudiates. Constant anger embitters man's life, makes him habitually irritable and relentless and unhappy. Now this tendency to anger was not given to man by God, for God, who is perfection, cannot be the source of human weaknesses; man does not create it himself, for he manifests it even before his conscious faculties come into action; it can be in his instinctive nature only as a transmission of the past.

Again, man exhibits his weaker self when he lends himself to envy. When he is steeped in envy, he is transformed into something inferior to himself. In his envy, man is unable to enjoy his own possessions because others possess more than he; he loses his ease because his neighbor enjoys comfort and abundance; he grows lean at the fatness of others, he grows miserable at the joys of others. The envious cannot bear to hear his neighbor praised, he cannot bear to see him rise, he cannot tolerate his assent into a station superior to his own, he cannot brook his cheer and laughter. In his envy, man will commit the most absurd acts, he will seek to excite in his neighbor the state of mind in which he is himself. To this end, he will live in extravagant fashion, making a display of wealth which he does not possess; he will make pretentions of all kinds, and live under false colors. Such a manner of living, however, will prove hurtful only to himself. The mind wounded with envy no longer centers itself on the vital issues of life, it ceases to identify itself with the deeper human interests, it ceases to create and to meet important problems. It is envious and therefore keeps itself occupied in watching the advance of others. Although such a vigilance only brings more and more hurt unto himself, yet he persists and augments his own misery. The envious man can see nothing of good in those he envies; he will magnify their deficiencies, exaggerate their faults, misinterpret and misrepresent their every act. Surely this vicious tendency in the human heart was not given by God, for the Almighty and the All-Perfect, who has lovingly brought man into existence, could not have implanted such a weakness in His creature. Man himself did not create it, he finds it in his consciousness but does not plant it there. In fact, man himself does not know the stuff of which envy is made, or why he should find himself a prey to envy. Envy therefore is but another transmission from the past.

Man again lends himself to his weaker self when he allies himself with pessimism, when he sinks his mind below the level of hopefulness, when he steeps his heart in worry and fear, when he retires from a world of cheer and beauty and sunshine into one of gloominess and despair. A pessimistic outlook upon life has brought much misery to man; it has beclouded his countenance, it has dimmed his vision, it has soured his heart, weakened his organs, disturbed his functions, slackened his motions, lowered his vitality and interfered with his efforts. When the pessimistic self is active, man ceases to be himself, he ceases to see things as they are. The sun ceases to shine for him, the beauty of nature, the glory of the world is not at all perceived, the days move sluggishly and colorlessly. Life becomes a weariness. Worry and fear crush out all its joy. But how have worry and fear come into existence? Here too we may say these pernicious tendencies trace their inception to the past. God, our Father, full of love for His children, surely did not instil in them this unhappiness; man himself fosters these evils, develops them, gives them harbor in his heart, but he does not create them. They have existed long before he came into existence, they were here long before he made his appearance in the world. They are therefore the creations of the past.

Here we must distinguish between what we call transmissions of the past and heredity. They are apparently the same, but fundamentally different. When we speak of heredity we mean the tracing of certain characteristics or capabilities to one or both parents. But when we speak of the transmissions of the past, we mean the remote past, the racial past, the characteristics and peculiarities developed by mankind in the process of its growth and development, which the members of each generation equally share.

But man must free himself, and can free himself, from those deeply transmitted weaknesses. That which God has created is everlasting and man cannot overthrow it, but that which man has created man can also destroy. Orders, systems, ranks, thrones, which man instituted and served, are now overthrown because man of today recognizes their futility and their harm.

If man can work fundamental changes in his outer world, why should he not be able to effect similar changes in his inner world? If he has succeeded in overthrowing the tyrants of his freedom after they had reigned for countless generations, why should we doubt his power to overthrow this inner tyranny of the past? If he has banished the enemies of liberty, why should he not also banish the foes of his happiness and peace of mind?

But how? How can we dislodge our inner enemies? Let me say, first of all, that we must pitch a battle against the enemies within with as much earnestness and zeal and energy as we would against the enemies without. Whoever would make this fight, let him determine not to leave the field of battle until victorious. Then let him develop the positive elements of his disposition with which to combat the weakly, negative manifestations.

How to fight anger? First, by developing serenity. The more you train yourself to act serenely, the more you cultivate poise and tranquility, the more do you weaken the ascendency of anger. When you act serenely, your reason and your judgment are free to act, and

when these are in action, your anger has little
chance to rise. Again, when it does rise, give
it no expression; do not speak when in an angry
mood, do not give orders to your employees, do
not transact business, do not go out to see
friends when anger possesses you. Needless to
say, do not speak to your wife or to your children at such moments, but pause and wait until
the tempest within you ceases to rage. When
anger finds no field for expression in you, no
outlet for its fury, it will cease to torment you;
it will leave your being.

In the same manner, you can destroy envy in
yourself. Cultivate first its positive aspect in
your consciousness. Cultivate contentment. Develop the habit of affirming "Thank God for
what I have."   Be happy with your good
health, with your life companion, with your
children, with your friends, with the brightness
of the sun, with each day as it comes; for
each day is a glorious possession, if you but
enjoy it. And then, should envy venture into
the threshold of your consciousness, stifle it by
repeating "Love thy neighbor as thyself,"
which implies: take delight in his comfort as
you do in your own. Give your envy no ears,

give it no eyes, lend it no tongue, and it will retreat, defeated.

You can also annihilate a worrisome mood, a pessimistic outlook upon life. Cultivate faith and hopefulness. Affirm repeatedly: "I trust in God's help, I know that everything will be for the best." Wear a cheerful countenance; in the apparently darkest hours, smile; in the face of apparent calamity, stand at a distance and watch patiently, for calamity never lasts. Even floods must cease, and they leave the soil more fertile for growth. In the face of calamity, do as much as you can with your faculties, with your toil, with your will, but nothing with your mood; for the mood is treacherous, it can obstruct vision, paralyze action, and stifle aspiration. Cultivate a sane, salutary optimism and you will emerge from all calamities unhurt.

We can change thus the destructive currents of the past, we can barricade ourselves against them. And in cleansing ourselves from the evils impinged on us by the past, we may bear in mind that we are not only aiding ourselves, but laying the cornerstone of a better life for our children. Just as our life is the direct cause of their existence, so does our conduct and our habits greatly determine their conduct and their reactions. By battling and conquering the foes of the past, by turning away at the gate the enemies of the human heart, we prepare for our children a world of brighter days and happier years. If our forefathers had arrayed themselves in battle against the inner destroyers of happiness, if they had destroyed from within themselves worry and anger and fear, we to-day would have been better equipped to enjoy the blessings of life. We must do that which our ancestors failed to do. We must aim to transmit to our posterity a past of serenity, of contentment, of hope and of optimism; then both we and they, shall realize God's blessings on earth.

THE POWER OF THOUGHT

All tangible reality is the incarnation of thought. This civilization of ours is the off-spring of man's Thought; the universe is the expression of Divine Thought. As we look about us we see countless man-made structures towering skyward, flawless in design, superb in their solidity. How have they come into existence? They are the actualization of thoughts. Before these lofty skyscrapers took visible form, they were conceived in someone's mind, completed there in their minutest detail before a single stone was laid. They would never have come into being, if they had not first been born in someone's thoughts. The countless conveniences of modern life, the many uses of electricity, the telegraph, the telephone, the wireless, the radio. How have these systems sprung into existence? They were first created in thought, and then became realities. Likewise the man-made beauties of life; sculptures, paintings, and all other art; governmental systems, educational methods, industrial orders, all the complex and multifarious institutions which together form the network of modern civilization, were created first in someone's mind.

Every existing thing is the expression of Thought. Man-made things are the expression of man's thought; all else and man himself, is the expression of Divine Thought. The entire solar and planetary system; the sun, the moon, the stars, the clouds, the rivers, mountains, valleys, trees, flowers and birds; all, all are expressions of thought. And just as these creations transcend infinitely the work of man, so naturally must the mind in which they originated transcend the mind of man. The universe is the expression of the Universal Mind, —of God.

The human mind, however, does not differ from the Universal Mind in essence or in aspiration; for in both instances we see the same intense urge towards expression, towards creation. The shortcomings of the human mind lie in its finiteness, as well as in its inability to transplant itself into the thing it creates. What do we mean when we say it is incapable of transplanting itself into the thing it creates?

The human mind first forms a mental image of the thing it creates, then brings it forth into visible reality. But after that, the relationship between the creating mind and the thing created ceases. Once the edifice has been erected, all affinity between itself and the architect who created it is severed. It becomes independent of the mind which created it. It is otherwise with those things that are created by the Universal Mind. There is *no* cessation of relationship and influence between the Universal Mind and the thing it creates. The Universal Mind resides in the very things it creates, almost as if the things were created in order to extend its habitation. The thing that the Universal Mind creates begins to grow and develop and gain, from the moment it appears on earth; for it contains a vital principle that makes for growth and development; it is inhabited by divine power. The products of the human mind, on the other hand, enter into a process of decay from the moment of their creation. Do not think that a building becomes dilapidated at a particular stage of existence; the process of decay really sets in immediately upon its erection, from the moment it becomes exposed to heat and cold and time. The torrents of rain, the biting blasts, are forces that refresh the creations of the Universal Mind, but they are dangerous to the products of the human mind. This is because the Universal Mind transplants itself into the things it creates, while the human mind cannot. What man creates is a mechanism, what God creates is an organism.

But whatever the shortcomings of the human mind when compared to the Universal Mind, in its own sphere it is the only reality, the only sentient and creative power that we possess. It is the mind that perceives, it is the mind that interprets facts, it is the mind that composes and creates new forms of reality. It is the mind that rejoices, it is the mind that suffers, it is the mind that feels sorrow or pain. Everything in man begins at the center, that is, in the mind, and grows from inside out. Do not think that circumstances in themselves have the power to make us miserable. No! Our surroundings would never disturb us if we did not first interpret and picture them in our minds as frightful monsters.

We are just beginning to realize that right

thinking is the key to health and success; and right thinking in turn is the result of a conscious effort to perceive the soft, beautiful aspects of reality. There have been souls in this world who by nature were able to perceive nothing but the beautiful, tender lines of life; but their numbers have been few. The general individual comes to such a view-point only through a conscious effort to discard all that is petty and insignificant in his experience, to see things with unblurred vision and unfettered imagination. When we shall learn to perceive the broader outlines of our being, when we shall learn to see ourselves in relation to the universe, in relation to the eternal life, in relation to the universal mind, we shall then truly come to behold the great significance of our own life.

Thought is given to man in a potential state, and it is its nature to grow and develop in the direction in which it is led. Lead your thought on the tracks of meanness and revenge, and your thought will continue of its own accord to lead *you* on that road. Whenever it will detect an opportunity for base action it will seize upon it and utilize it until it is full-fed. The result for you can be only misery and unhappiness. On the other hand, habituate your thought to perceive the goodness and benevolence permeating this world, and it will always pause at a deed or manifestation of goodness; it will nurture itself upon it, and bring you a great meed of happiness. Show your thought the way to anxiety and it will always find some cause for worry. It will torture itself with anxieties until the very foundations of health will be undermined. On the other hand, set your thought on the joyous, hopeful path and it will eschew worry and fear as by instinct; it will establish itself firmly in the citadel of hope and joy. And what of health thoughts and thoughts of sickness? Think of sickness all the time, brood over your past and present pains, and without a doubt your ailments will multiply. You will find yourself seeking out the companionship of those who also can speak of their diseases and who will listen to the lengthy enumeration of your own. The constant reiteration of your unhappy condition will have its effect on your body in continued and even increased ailments. Think instead of health, and you will find yourself drawn to healthy people, you will find your own ailments receding, your body will respond by sloughing off the real and imaginary ills in which your thoughts had dwelt.

The shrine of thought is entrusted to our will. We have it in us to consecrate it or desecrate it, to make it shine forth with magnificent radiance or become a deleterious instrument. Thought is the only true reality there is, the only reality that constitutes man and God; and all realities are the expression of this true reality. We have it in our power to make this reality one of joy and happiness. "As a man thinketh so is he." Let our thought be always in the direction of happiness and health, faith and serenity; and let us shut the door of our mind tight against misery, doubt and ill-health.

PRIDE AND VANITY

We read in the Old Testament many admonitions against pride and vanity. The Book of Proverbs, in particular, contains much reproof of the vain and the proud. And we may add to these the words of moralists and sages of subsequent generations, who likewise rail against these failings. Pride and vanity are two weaknesses of human nature from which man must purify himself if he would attain the highest expression of himself.

Pride and vanity, like all other human failings, brings injury only to the one who harbors them. The bitterest enemies of man are not outside of himself, they are within himself. How often may it be said of one whose life has proved a sad failure: "His greatest enemy was himself!" No enemy from without will do man as much harm in a year as, let us say, an outburst of anger on his part will do him in an hour. His bitterest foe cannot cut so deeply and so ferociously at the root of his health as will an inner attack of worry and fear, or the constant gnawing of envy and discontent. And no slander, no calumny will so vitiate his name in the eyes of his fellow-men, as will his own vanity and pride.

Vanity and pride are both exaggerated states of self-love; they both enormously accentuate the self. Those who are obsessed by these two vices have no eyes for the rest of the world, for their vision is uninterruptedly centered on the self.

Though often synonymously used, yet there is a marked distinction between pride and vanity. Pride is self-admiration, while vanity seeks the admiration of others; the proud man places an exaggerated value on himself, a vain man seeks unduly the applause of the world.

Leaving aside for a moment the weakness of vanity, and considering that of pride, let us, first of all, not confuse self-pride with self-respect. Self-respect is a great virtue, and has no relation to self-pride. Self-respect is a religious trait, whether consciously so or not. He who possesses self-respect has, in reality, respect for his divine self. He respects the divine gifts that are his; he has respect for his faculties, for his organs, for his powers, for his man-

hood, for every other endowment that God lavished upon him. He respects himself not because he considers himself superior to others,
but because he realizes that something divine is
encased in his heart, he senses that something
divine is entrenched in his mind, he sees his
whole being as an emanation from the Infinite
Source of life; his respect is for the Divine
Presence that is within him. He who has respect for himself, also cherishes respect for
others, for he perceives in others the same
divine gifts that he finds in himself. Self-pride,
on the other hand, is an irreligious attitude towards life. The proud man does not see himself as the recipient of divine gifts. Whatever
he has is his, and whatever he is is better than
what others are. He therefore assumes an
aloofness from the rest of his kind.

This attitude of pride and aloofness is injurious to man's development and happiness,
because it is erroneous and contrary to the
divine nature within him. God did not create
aristocrats in this world; these are self-made.
In fact, if we reflect upon the eternal forces of
nature, the great messengers of the Divine
Mind, we immediately see that aloofness and

discrimination are entirely foreign to their law
and character.   Nature is absolutely modest
and democratic.   The sun sends its beams upon
the cottage as upon the palace, it warms the
poor as well as the rich.   The moon sheds its
radiance upon all races, upon all nations, upon
all men.   The flowers give their beauty and
their scent to all, the trees offer their shade and
their shelter to all, the atmosphere gives of its
invigorating freshness to all. We see that God,
in His creation, has made no distinction between one race and another, between one man
and another.   This assumption of aloofness
and pride, therefore, is arbitrary and false; it
is contrary to the will of God and a violation
of the inherent democracy of nature.

What is worse, pride, which combines excessive self-love with a disregard for others, is a
snare to the proud; for instead of enhancing
their happiness, their seclusiveness and aloofness become a source of great unhappiness.
Because meekness and democracy are the
methods of nature and the ways of God, mankind, too, loves meekness and democracy, and
detests haughtiness and aloofness.   The world
treats the individual in the very same manner

in which the individual treats the world. It smiles at him whose countenance is charged with cheer; it frowns to him whose brow is constantly overcast with gloom. In a sense, the world is the mirror of our soul; in the world's reaction to us, we can become conscious of our own reaction towards it. The soul that loves everyone, receives love from everyone, while the soul that is embittered against everyone is the recipient of bitterness from everyone; the soul that is modest and sympathetic to everyone, receives the praise and sympathy of everyone, while the heart that is proud and indifferent to the rest of the world, becomes the object of indifference and disdain among men. For this reason, the proud have but few friends, they find themselves lonely and alone. Of course, they see that the fault lies with this base world around them, but it is they alone who build this barrier between themselves and the rest of mankind.

As we study the history of the human character, however, we learn that the more enlightened the age, the less high is the barrier of pride between men and between groups; we learn that it is only in epochs where ignorance dominates, that pride and its social consequences are rampant. In the semi-civilized eras of antiquity, we find extreme discriminations between group and group, between class and class, between man and man. Before the rise of civilization, we saw the dominance of castes,—the castes of proud nobles, proud patricians, proud priests, proud knights, proud kings; but civilization is constantly levelling the arbitrary heights between man and man, it is constantly puncturing the inflated pride of class to which groups and families have tried to cling, it is constantly bringing man nearer and nearer to his fellow-man. And although today we still find the proud rich, although we still find undefined social classes, these too are being constantly eliminated and discarded. Civilization has weakened the strongholds of the proud.

But while civilization, on the one hand, has discouraged the existence of pride, particularly that which expresses itself in undemocratic relations among men, it has, on the other hand, encouraged the growth of vanity in man's nature. Pride, we said, is the admiration that one has for oneself; vanity is the admiration

that one seeks from others. It is pitiful, almost,
to see how eagerly men and women seek the
esteem of their neighbors, how dearly they are
willing to pay for the good opinion of their
fellow-beings. In their manner, in their speech,
in their clothes, in their home, in the least
significant as well as the most important matters of life, they are constantly subjecting
themselves to the opinion of others. We are
all too eager for this good opinion, and we are
thereby doing ourselves an injury; for, more
and more, we are losing thereby our individuality. We are becoming more and more affec-
tatious, we are becoming more and more
pretentious, more and more ostentatious, and
we are losing more and more our simple,
natural self, our genuine, simple demeanor. We
are building a duality in our nature, we are
creating a double self in ourselves—one self
for the home and one for the street, one self
for the family and one for society; and these
selves being so different one from the other—
one genuine and the other pretentious, one
simple and the other making a boastful appearance—work great harm in our nature, and
make our lives uneasy and restless; this un-

natural duality deprives us of quietude and peace of mind.

It is a peculiar thing that human nature should, on the one hand, seek greater freedom, and on the other hand, throw itself into bondage. On the one hand, man has overthrown his enslavers, dragged down his tyrants, destroyed his kings, and on the other hand, he has voluntarily enslaved himself to the opinion of society. He outdoes himself and spends himself and even suffers acutely in order to satisfy the opinion of society. What is worse, all these unnatural efforts on his part to gain the good opinion of others, are futile. For the eye of the world is exceedingly keen, it knows what is of true worth and what is not. To gain the genuine appreciation of the world, one must do something valuable for the world. Let one give expression not to his pretended self, but to his true self and the world will cherish his deeds. Let man give expression to his natural goodness, to his unaffected tenderness, and the world will not be slow to appreciate these qualities; let a man benefit mankind by his love, by his sympathies, and mankind will erect immortal monuments to his name. Let man be his true self, his natural divine self, and he will not need to seek the high opinion of his neighbors; it will be his without the seeking.

Pride and vanity, these two weaknesses of human nature, are among the most insalubrious influences of man's life. But man has the power to tower above them, to eradicate them from his consciousness. He can conquer pride by realizing the divine intention of democracy among men as among the elements of nature; he can conquer vanity by living a simple, genuine and modest life, true to himself and the divine nature within himself.

PEACE OF MIND

Peace dwells unshakably in the heart of man as it dwells in the heart of nature. In the external universe there is ceaseless turmoil, change, unrest, turbulence; in the heart of things there is undisturbed repose. The surface of the ocean may be lashed by wind and wave, but no storm can penetrate the tranquil heart of the sea. There is a calmness in the center of all nature; in the field, in the river, in the hill, in the valley, in the mountain, in the heart of the forest, in all creation. And this divine serenity dwells also in the heart of man, who is himself the heart of creation. There is an inner tranquility, an inner silence that is not disturbed by the agitation and fermentation of life's stern combats, that is not moved either by the smiles or the frowns of fortune, that is not affected by sickness or sorrow. This divine tranquility resides in the innermost chamber of the heart; it is the resting place of God. When this manifests itself in its fullness, projecting itself into the conscious self, man experiences peace of mind.

Peace of mind means perfect harmony between the various elements that constitute man; harmony between the forces within and the forces without. It implies the unity of man. It means that he expresses one individuality in all his relations of life. There is no division between his thought and his tongue, between his heart and his lips. When man does not permit the experiences and exigencies of the outer life to overlay the tranquility within, he has achieved peace of mind.

Peace of mind is prerequisite to happiness. Happiness enters only through the channel of the mind. Happiness is a subjective, never an objective, state. If the mind, the receptive organ, is in a chaotic, disturbed condition, happiness cannot penetrate it, though every outward circumstance may favor it. To many, indeed, peace of mind is identified with happiness. At any rate, it is surely a foundation without which happiness cannot for a moment exist.

Love, too, can flourish only on a serene background; it can bloom and blossom only in a placid, peaceful atmosphere, in an abundance of sunshine. There can be no true love in a mind that is not at peace with itself; restlessness distorts the power of love, it perverts its functions; it infects it with its own uneasiness and changes its nature. Love that is nurtured in a turbulent state of mind no longer elevates the faculties, no longer stimulates the soul, no longer with its subtle power expands the emotions and fills them with new vitality and tender joy; but it breaks out like a raging sea, like a passionate whirlwind bent only on destruction.

Peace of mind is essential to achievement and accomplishment. No great work was ever achieved in hours of excitation or agitation, no monumental task was ever completed by a mind at war with itself. Read the biographies of the great men of the ages and you will find that flashes of genius burst forth from the mind only in its calm and serene moments, when all the turmoil of the world outside is hushed. The masterpieces which illumine the path of mankind are the offspring of serene vision and calm judgment. But why allude to immortal works? We experience this in our daily life, that our best work, the work that really counts, is produced when our inner life is possessed of harmony and peace. We may work slowly or with great speed and even with intensity, but if a sense of calmness pervades us, a sense of peace with the world and with ourselves, we shall bring forth the best and the most that is within us.

We are well aware of the fact that there are forces to-day responsible for the disturbance of our serenity. There is worry, gnawing at the very roots of our being, twisting and perverting every small incident of life into a grotesque and gigantic misfortune, into foreboding of evil. There is fear assailing the finest fibers of our mind, paralysing action, hindering progress. There is sorrow casting its shadow on the brightness of life, enshrouding all existence with gloom. There is anger, pouring its poison into our system, diminishing our resistance, lowering our vitality, blurring our vision. There are all these deadly enemies striking daily at our peace of mind.

But all these forces are negative forces. They are not to be combated, they are to be replaced. Fill the mind with hope, and worry will flee, fill it with courage, and fear will disappear, fill it with cheer, and sorrow will take wings, fill it with goodwill, and anger will draw in its fangs. We achieve, or rather restore, our natural peace of mind by substituting the positive forces of life for the negative forces that have found entrance in our mind.

But the great problem is how, how to do it, how to obtain hope and courage and cheer and goodwill. Study the life of a man from his childhood up and you will see that worry, bitterness, gloom enter the heart of man from the moment only that he begins to depend on himself alone in making his way through life, or as some people would prefer to put it, from the moment he becomes *independent*. The child, while under the care of his parents, knows neither worry, anxiety nor gloom; his natural cheerfulness and joy finds constant expression; he avoids sorrow as he would danger; he has no forebodings of evil or misfortune; he is not afraid of the future, and, unless the poison of prejudice has been early instilled in him, his little heart is full of love and good-will towards everyone about him. All the time that he is utterly dependent upon his parents, his life is free from care and anxiety, and filled

with joy and cheer and *peace*. He lives the
life intended for all mankind, if mankind would
but realize the divine intention and follow it.
A child is happy and *free*, because he is dependent. He is dependent upon his parents,
and has utter faith in them. He knows that
they will supply him with sustenance and pro-
vide for all his wants; he knows that their
love enfolds him like wings and that he can
never stray from its warmth; he knows that no
matter what his difficulties, his desires, his
wrong-doings even, they will be ready always
to help and guide and comfort and forgive.
His life is then perfect, for in the realization of
and dependence upon his parents' love and sustenance, only the positive forces of life find expression. It is only when he leaves childhood
and dependence behind him, when he begins to
feel the burdens of life singly upon his should-
ers, when he feels that he has only himself to
turn to in moments of stress and exigency, that
the portals of his mind begin to open to the
negative forces of life,—to worry, anxiety, fear.

If man would but realize, when he frees himself from parental care, that he is still under
the care and protection of a Divine Father, to

Whose love he may turn at any moment, at any exigency of his life, he could retain unmarred the joy and peace that were his in his childhood. If man would but realize that he does not *need* to shoulder his burdens alone, that there is One who is ready to share them with him, nay, even to shoulder them for him, he would not be filled with forebodings for the future, with wretched doubt as to his ability to carry on the tasks required of him. If man would but lay aside his imagined independence, that is, his reliance upon himself alone, and recapture the dependence of his childhood, only this time not a dependence upon human devotion, but dependence on the one infallible Source of all Good, he would not need to lose, with the oncoming of maturity, the freedom and happiness and peace that are his birthright.

We must all know and live by the truth that God is with us and within us to help and guide and watch over us day and night, all the days of our life. We need but turn to Him, His light will shine upon us. We need but to hold out our hand and a strong Hand will lift us out of our difficulties. "The Lord is a shield about us," sang the Psalmist; "the Lord is my fortress. The Lord is my light and my salvation, whom shall I fear?" When your difficulties are too great, when your lot is more than you can bear, don't battle with your anxieties; put everything into the hands of God, He will make your woes to vanish, He will never fail you. Do you but call upon Him. Faith in God, *dependence* upon God—these are the only roads to harmony of being, to perfect and permanent peace of mind.

Be not misled by theories which teach that man is but a mechanical organism, that he is but a self-starting machine, that his life is but a transient shadow, that his mind is but a dream. No. Man is a reality. He is a shrine wherein Godly powers are stored. Man's powers are testimony of the Divine Power, man's mind is a spark of the Divine Mind, it is a ray of light emanating from an infinite luminary, and therefore a very part of it. If man would but see himself in this light, if he would but look upon himself as a part of divinity, all disturbance, all fear, all fright, all anxiety would flee from his existence.

Not material abundance, therefore, not fame,

not honor, not conquest, can of themselves bring peace of mind. The realization of material desires is not of necessity accompanied by peace of mind. The poor long for wealth, and think that in the achievement of wealth they will find peace. But do not the wealthy worry in spite of the plenty that surrounds them? The humble among mankind long perhaps for renown, for the achievement of heroic deeds. But do not the men of renown make themselves miserable despite the acclaim that is theirs? Do not heroes sink into gloom despite their glory? It is only he who is fortified with faith, be he rich or poor, great or humble, that preserves peace of mind.

The Psalmist and the Prophets who revealed Judaism to the world, taught God as a living God. They did not preach nor teach mere religious abstractions. God was very close to them. They spake to Him, and He spake to them. They *felt* the God power within them. They realized it with all their mind and heart. God to them was the only reality, the only light, the only power, the only source of goodness, the only fountain of joy. The God of the prophets and the Psalmist is also our God;

He has not changed; He is the same today as He was yesterday. We too can speak to Him, as the prophets did. But we, too, must *feel* His presence. We must open our hearts to Him, we must surrender ourselves to His care, deliver ourselves to His protection, truly trust in Him and hope in Him. With such faith, we, too, can reach loftier planes of existence, the very heights of happiness. With such faith, and with such faith only, can we achieve peace of mind.

THE DISTANCE TO PERFECTION

We recognize the calibre of an individual by his aspirations. The true man strives for perfection. The true artist has an image of perfection which he strives to bring into reality; he is not interested in compensation, only in the materializing of that perfect image. To the true man of letters, reward is an exceedingly remote thought, his life interest is in achieving perfection in the portrayal of his characters. The true builder does not build houses merely with the rental in mind, he first of all desires to build comfortable, lasting homes for men and women to dwell in. The true man refuses to identify himself with the insignificant aspects of reality, he craves always for that distant ideal which he sees as perfection.

Perfection is divine in its nature and in its origin. God Himself is making His world more and more perfect. He is constantly evolving it from lower to higher states. He is constantly moulding it and refining it, and is steadily issuing forth forms of greater beauty, beings of superior endowment, better equipped, better able to preserve themselves. When man strives for perfection, he becomes God-like; he rises in his soul to greater heights and to greater freedom; he relinquishes more and more his mundane realm and enters into a state of spiritual happiness.

Of course, we must realize that perfection in itself is an abstraction, that is to say, perfection can be thought of only in connection with some reality. We can speak of attaining a perfect state, of performing a task in a perfect manner, of striving to make of ourselves perfect men; in all instances, we understand by perfection the reaching out for the best as applied to some specific reality. There is another characteristic attaching to perfection. And that is, that it is never attained. Although man strives for perfection, although he struggles and even suffers for it, yet it is never reached; it never, in fact, lends itself to realization. There is no standard by which perfection is measured, there is no specific height whereon it rests, so that one scaling that height would attain it. It has no specific distance, it is not marked by a specific goal. It is in the nature of perfection to keep its distance from man; the desire to attain it animates man, it stimulates him, but, like the horizon, it recedes to greater and greater distances as you travel to meet it. For this reason no man has ever attained perfection. When one makes the effort and conquers certain heights in life, he can only see from that top greater elevations to be reached; and when these are attained, there come into view still loftier extensions, greater altitudes; and when these, in turn, are scaled, man finds himself at the foot of still another magnificent and gigantic slope.

It is the unattainability of perfection that is the greatest blessing to those who are panting after it. Let no one be discouraged from pursuing it, because of inability to reach the goal. Let no one say to himself: "I cannot be perfect; no man has ever attained perfection. Why, then, need I struggle, why then need I master myself, why curb my appetites, and restrain my desires and make sacrifices to promote the good, when I realize that the ultimate good cannot at all be attained?" That perfection cannot be attained is not cause for discouragement and distress; on the contrary, it is cause for greater hope, deeper vision and higher happiness. Had man been able to attain perfection within the limited span of his years, his life would become exceedingly narrow, exceedingly circumscribed. He would then know that he was capable of doing so much and no more, that his reach could attain only to such and such a height, but no higher, that his whole life lay within certain narrow confines, beyond which he could not move. And when he had, let us say, reached that restricted elevation, what then? Then his life would become a dull monotony, with no horizon before him, his days would settle themselves into a monotonous and distressing procession; the period of striving and aspiring and hoping would be brief, the powers of his mind would have little or nothing more to do, for they would then have reached the zenith in their creativeness and their development. But with perfection always at a distance, life is always filled with meaning. The faculties find more work and finer work before them, the heart beats with hope in the anticipation of endless attainments; the world becomes larger, its opportunities for growth more numerous.

Man feels that his mission in life is a vital one, for it is an endless one and there is always more before him to do than he has already done. Man has therefore cause to rejoice daily that the perfection that beckons to him from the distance and stirs him to his greatest endeavors, is always beyond the horizon.

Perfection, we have said before, is only an abstraction and can be conceived only in conjunction with some phase of reality. While perfection should be sought for in every achievement, in every task, in every creative human effort, yet man should seek, above all, to render *himself* perfect. Man should strive to conquer the weaknesses, to master the frailties in his disposition; he should lead himself, train himself, just as he would endeavor to train his own child. Perfection in man implies both repression and expression. A man must repress in himself that which he condemns in others, or that which after doing, he regrets; on the other hand, he should impel himself to express that which he considers admirable in others, and that in which he himself delights after it is accomplished. And this is not an easy task. It means, first of all, constant vigilance, constant watchfulness over one's desires, thoughts, motives and reactions. It means a struggle—a struggle with unwholesome tendencies, with pressing instincts, with noxious habits, with ravenous appetites, with greedy desires, with unfavorable environment, with selfishness; and this struggle is all the more complex, because one must struggle with the very substance out of which one is made, one must grapple with the very mind out of which the wholesome thoughts also flow, with the very heart in which the noble impulses are also born. But if one emerges victorious, then his true manhood is triumphant and he will find himself far on the glowing road that he has set out to traverse.

The Sacred Scriptures enjoin us to seek perfection. The prophets, the priests, the sages, all preach to us to seek perfection for the self. All the divine messengers, all religions, endeavor to show the road that leads to self-perfection. Self-perfection is the ultimate duty of man. No tower can be greater than the height that man can build within himself, no treasures that he may amass can be richer than those of heart and disposition, no achievement can compare with that of achieving in himself the image of God.

In Leviticus we find the injunction: "Love the Lord thy God." To love the Lord, our God, means to love perfection, for He is perfect. He is both the source and the ideal of perfection. "Love Him with all thy heart, with all thy soul and with all thy might," for when you love, you seek to identify yourself with the one you love. Love Him, therefore, and you identify yourself with perfection.

THE POWER OF GOODNESS

The human personality is possessed of two distinct powers: the power of thought and the power of feeling. Thought was given to man chiefly for the purpose of self-preservation; that he may find sustenance, that he may build for himself a place of shelter, that he may discover the laws and the treasures of nature, that he may attain an intelligent understanding of his environment and be brought closer to the world in which he is placed. *Feeling* was lavished upon man chiefly in order that he may attune himself to mankind, that he may establish a sympathetic relationship with those of his kind, that he may co-operate and strive together with his fellow-man.

Psychology divides and subdivides human feelings, but we shall dwell, at this moment, upon only one—the feeling of kindness or goodness of heart. At no time does man appear so divine as when he gives expression to kindness. We know God through His kindness. God's presence is made manifest in many ways,

—in unceasing creation, in unfathomable wisdom, in eternal law and order. But these divine attributes do not reach the human understanding immediately; man needs first to reflect upon them, to ponder over them, before he can comprehend them. Not so with the divine attribute of kindness. Divine benevolence overwhelms man's understanding; life, health, strength, healing, love, hope, abundance all are divine gifts lavished upon man through the goodness of God, and without them man could not exist. God is thus known to man through His constantly expressed attribute of kindness. And we say that man appears God-like, when he too expresses himself in kindness.

The Talmud counts goodness of heart as the greatest of all virtues. Not justice, not righteousness, not courage, not refinement, not faithfulness, not truthfulness, but goodness of heart is the greatest of all the virtues; for the heart that is good contains them all, the heart that is good cherishes them all, practices them all; the heart that is good is just and righteous and courageous and refined and faithful and truthful. It is the goodness of the human heart that has sought again and again to preserve humanity; it is the goodness in the human heart that has been working untiringly to eliminate suffering, to ameliorate evil conditions, to establish institutions that help and elevate, that battle with want and poverty, that extend aid to the wounded and the weak and the helpless. We may well maintain, therefore, that the biological theory that claims the survival of the fittest through the struggle for existence, cannot be entirely correct. Struggle alone would have put a stop to every heart beat, it would have silenced every pulse, it would have devastated the species. Generations have survived and moved onward, not through struggle but through cooperation, not through brutal courage and the expression of a selfish will but through the expression of a gentle heart; through kindness, tenderness and benevolence.

Goodness of heart must express itself in two ways, one of which is positive and the other negative. On its positive side, goodness demands self-abnegation, self-denial, self-surrender. By this I mean that while goodness is the property of every human heart, yet it is not always properly directed and not always suitably applied.

Goodness is very often applied only to the self. The individual is good to himself. His attention and his interest are centered chiefly on his self; he watches himself, cherishes himself, is wholly absorbed in himself. Here you have goodness misdirected, kindness perverted, fine energy utilized for the augmentation of selfishness. Altruistic goodness can forget the self, and, if necessary, even deny the self, and give to others not less care than it gives to itself. Good souls are those that make room in their spaciousness for other souls. Good hearts are those that seek out other hearts upon whom to lavish of their tenderness and helpfulness. Truly good men and women are only those who feel the woes and miseries of their fellows and who, without delay and without personal motive, apply themselves to their alleviation. To the good there occurs no question as to station, no partiality to rank or wealth. To them humanity is one. The good not only show sympathy but *are* sympathetic; to them compassion is not an act of convention or propriety, but an act of the emotions, welling up from the very depths of consciousness. These men and women increase manifold the happiness of mankind; they cheer with their look, encourage with their word, kindle hope with their smile, banish misery with their optimistic gesture, support and sustain with their generosity. These are the stronghold and the blessing of mankind.

I said that goodness has also a negative aspect. The positive aspect of goodness is contained in the injunction of the Old Testament, "Love thy neighbor as thyself," that is to say, do unto him as you would do unto yourself, feel for him as you do for yourself, cherish him as you do yourself. The negative aspect of goodness is stated in the Talmud by Hillel, thus: "That which is objectionable unto thyself, do not do unto thy neighbor." The positive aspect deals with that which you should do, and the negative aspect with that which you should not do unto your neighbor. The positive is essentially an expression of love, the negative is fundamentally an expression of justice. To do good is indeed the highest ideal, but before man attains this height, he must first learn not to do harm. "That which is *objectionable* unto thee, do not do unto thy neighbor." The negative is as vital as the positive. In fact, it clears the road, it makes it possible for the positive to enter and assert itself.

We live in an age of competition, in an age where in each field, be that of industry, or commerce or even the professions, each one is racing with his fellow-beings. Each one is endeavoring to outdo the other, to defeat the other and capture the field for himself. Men are constantly engaged in a deadly struggle, grappling with one another, striking and tearing and stifling each other. In this competition, hardness and indifference develop in the individual. The heart grows cold, the mind becomes one-sided, the jaw becomes set, the eyes see the world only as a running field in which the individual is a runner bent only on reaching the goal post. It is needless to say that in such a state of things, goodness suffers greatly, sympathy becomes deeply wounded, kindness, tenderness, compassion become faint to the vanishing point, the positive as well as the negative aspects of goodness are constantly violated, and humanity is indeed the loser.

What then? Are we to withdraw from life? Or are we to overlook those who struggle against us? No, you need not retire from life, but instead of facing it with a combative attitude, face it with a creative attitude. Instead of keeping your eyes fixed on what others do, keep your eyes and attention fixed on your own task; instead of endeavoring to do better than others, do the best that is in you, and the best in you will always receive its reward. The energy wasted in competition, the thought squandered in the competitive struggle, the disquietude, the anxiety, the bitterness involved,—if this energy were engaged in creative achievement, the accomplishment would be so much greater, and life so much better. There is moreover a great ethical difference between saying "This line of mine is better than that of others," and "In this line I am at my best." In the latter, man preserves his goodness. A man can be a good business man, and still be a good man. He can add not only to his fortune, but also to the happiness of his kind.

Goodness is at least as important to humanity as industry. The progress of the human heart must not be less than the progress of the human mind. With his mind, man brings comfort and convenience to the world, but it is with his heart that he brings happiness. Just as man is compensated for his industry, so is he even more rewarded for his goodness. A good deed is never lost, a kind act is never forgotten. Goodness gives birth to goodness, it creates, it stimulates goodness in others, and thus goes on, endless in its planting of happiness.

Goodness is rewarded on this very earth, the good need not wait for the hereafter to enjoy its gifts. For the good are never bitter, are never envious, they know joy and cheer and serenity; their life is a full one, and their days are many on this earth.

A FRIEND

What is a friend? A friend is one that takes our soul out of its seclusion and brings it into the open to breathe more freely and enjoy the open sun. It is one in whose presence our inner self relinquishes its deep place of concealment and makes its appearance on the very surface of our being. Before a friend we have no secret reservations, no hidden thoughts. In his presence there are no artificial restrictions, no fear of social infringement, no anxiety about unkind criticism or unfavorable reaction.

A friend is a trust. We trust him with our innermost feelings; we confide in him our most sacred thoughts. We trust him with our plans and our ambitions; we trust him with our aims and our hopes. Our friend stores away our private feelings; he locks up our secret thoughts in the very same shrine where his own are deposited; to him there is no division between our inner possessions and his own.

In a friend we find another self. He not only is the one to whom we can fully reveal ourselves, but he is also one who is ready to help us, to guide us, to counsel us. A true friend is never envious of our achievements, he is never jealous of our success. On the contrary, he takes pride in our accomplishments, he delights in our gain; for he identifies himself with us, and our attainments bring him the same joy as his own. A friend does not despise us for our weaknesses; he either condones them as he would his own, or sets out energetically though sympathetically to correct them. And he corrects them not in public, but in strict privacy. His interest in our perfection is not less than in his own, and in the preservation of our honor not less than in his own. Therefore he has respect for our sensibilities and does not expose them to public hurt. A true friend, however, does not flatter us; he does not praise us for qualities which we do not possess or for deeds we have never performed. He does not endeavor to present us with an erroneous and misleading likeness of our personality; he does not encourage our vanity in order to receive our favor. He will praise us, he will applaud us, but only when in his judgment we are worthy of praise and acclaim; he will then not refrain from an expression of his appreciation and will seek with it to spur us on in the continuation of worthiness.

Because a true friend is earnestly interested in our well-being, we can turn to him in every exigency. Life is not a straight, smooth road. There are times when fortune, at least temporarily, withdraws her favors from us; there are circumstances which threaten our welfare, our happiness. Then will that friend hold out his hand for our support; then will he make our burden lighter by helping us to carry it. Often his encouraging word, his optimistic gesture, his hopeful glance, his expression of confidence in our ability, is all that is necessary to help us disentangle ourselves from apparently strangling circumstances.

On our friend we can rely also in our sorrow. A friend knows how to console; he may not utter a single sound of solace, yet in his presence we become conscious of a world of eloquent pleas bidding us control our emotions and trust in God's goodness and mercy. In his presence, we feel a world of sympathy flowing out to us, enveloping us in its tenderness and compassion. We can also rely upon him in our joy. In our sorrow his feelings neutralize ours, but in our joy his feelings enhance ours. His joy at our joy augments our joy. He adds nourishment to our happy emotions, he adds vitality to our happy thoughts, he gives stability and permanence to the milestones of our joys.

It is clear that a true friend is an inestimable treasure, a veritable fortune. But how is friendship built? How is a friend begotten? No set of rules may be formulated by which friendship may be established or sustained. Friendship is not a business partnership which can be bound by agreements and regulations; it is not even a contract between two minds determined to be in close and frequent touch with one another. It is an unwritten compact between two hearts; it is an unexpressed, unceremonial union of kindred sympathies and spirits, it is a perfect harmonization between two personalities—an harmony which renders them obvious to possible differences and bends them more and more to each other.

How, again, is a friend made? A friend is made through friendship. We must do first for him what he later does for us. We receive his sympathy only after we have given him ours; we receive his care only after we have lavished upon him ours; we receive his compassion and devotion after we have tendered him ours; we receive his helping, sustaining hand after we have extended to him ours; we become a vital center of his interest, a cause for his self-denial and self-sacrifice only after he has come to mean just those things to us. Friendship is, unconsciously, a give-and-take process, we first give what is best in us and receive, in return, what is best in others. Friendship, however, flourishes best where tenderness and devotion are expressed disinterestedly—free from selfish intentions. By this I mean that the service and self-sacrifice which one may render to a fellow-man, should not be given with the preconceived purpose of receiving similar or greater benefits in return. Acts of kindness performed with an ulterior motive may call forth courtesy, but will not evoke friendship; they will make the recipient politely appreciative, but they will not touch the tenderest fibres in his heart. In friendship, there is a response of emotion to emotion, feelings are stirred by feelings; only what one gives of himself will he receive correspondingly from others. And one must give of himself not in order to receive this compensation, but because he desires the happiness of the other; his reward will come only indirectly and unsought. As a material investment, friendship may prove a disappointment, but as a spiritual expression of the self there are no greater returns.

Friendship, once established, must be nurtured and preserved. We must remember that in friendship there is not necessarily a blood relationship, which is indissoluble, nor an economical relationship, which is held together through motives of respective self-interest; in friendship, the relationship is purely emotional. Only the feelings are involved, and feelings are highly vulnerable. They are subject to injury or to starvation. A friendship, no matter how strongly intrenched, may be hurt, it may even be severed. A friend, once gained, must not be carelessly forfeited. Never ridicule a friend, even in jest; do not make your friend the object of your laughter; include him in your merriment, but do not make him the butt of your mirth. Mockery is not the expression of sympathy or of love. Neither should you criti-

cize a friend, merely for the sake of being critical. I say for the sake of being critical, for
criticism is not always the result of judgment,
but often merely the result of habit—of a critical habit. Such a habit is obnoxious, and particularly when it seeks a friend for its mark.
Do not make a friend in order to remake him;
do not make a friend in order to teach him or
correct him; your friendship must be based on
what he is, not on what he might be. In this
respect friendship is almost like marriage; in
marriage a man commits a serious error if he
takes a woman to himself in order to train
her; and so does a woman commit a similar
error who marries a man in order to "bring him
up." In either case, the result can only be constant clash and disagreement. A man does not
like to be the pupil of his wife, nor does a woman wish to have her husband for a school-
master. One must take the other just as she or
he is, without conscious attempt at reformation.
Of course, they do teach one another, they do
train one another, but not consciously; it takes
the form of a mutual unconscious influence,
which harmonious, sympathetic souls exercise
upon one another. In the same way, friends may

influence and inspire one another, but it cannot be carpingly or laboriously done; it must come naturally, quietly and without premeditation; the more unconscious the influence they exercise upon one another, the deeper and more lasting it will be.

Before a friend, we must guard ourselves against the expression of narrowness in our nature; neither narrow-mindedness nor narrow-heartedness must come to the surface. A friend must call forth only the finest elements in our being, and by constantly expressing these, and suppressing all petty impulses, any smallness in our nature will gradually be stamped out, leaving room for the expansion of our nobler selves.

To strengthen friendship, it is well to join a friend in the pursuit of an ideal. In true friendship, there is not only the element of mutual helpfulness, but also the bond of common idealism. Men become stauncher friends when they strive for the realization of the same ideal, when their minds meet on the same spiritual plane, striving both for the same spiritual aims. Then the higher the ideal, and the more strongly they are devoted to it, the more indissolubly will their friendship be intertwined with it.

In order to make a friend we must use tenderness, and in order to keep a friend, we must use care and judgment. And it is not difficult to understand why some have many friends, and others have none. Men and women of selfish tendencies have no friends. Those who see only themselves in the center of everything, those who see the rest of creation only in relation to their own wants and needs, those who think only of themselves, speak only of themselves, feel only their own woes, and are elated only over their own joys, these are destitute of friends. Since friendship is a give-and-take process, on a high plane, those who cannot give of themselves to others, can receive no friendliness from others; those whose minds are deeply engrossed in themselves, can only find coldness and indifference in others. In humanity, our own personality is reflected; in its relation to us, we can detect our relation to it. Humanity is not mean, it is not hardened, it is not indifferent, it is not inconsiderate; it is only compensatory. It gives us measure for measure, both in sympathy and in selfishness. Just as the sympathetic and the loving find themselves surrounded by hosts of friends, so the indifferent and the egotistic are left lonely and destitute.

There is none, however, that need be destitute of friends; for friendship is not the particular endowment of a choice few, everyone of us has the price required for the purchase of friendship. We all have a great deal more tenderness and sympathy than we give expression to, we all have more goodness, more devotion than we generally manifest. It is in us to express ourselves in deeds of kindness and devotion and thereby strengthen and cement our relations with our fellow men. We were created to live in fellowship and friendship with our kind, and all that is required is the exertion on our part, always richly rewarded, to meet the conditions of such association.

MY NEIGHBOR AND MYSELF

The greatest injunction of the Old Testament is "Love thy neighbor as Thyself." All the laws and commandments are included in this one. If you love your neighbor as yourself, you will not kill, you will not steal, you will not commit adultery; if you love your neighbor as yourself, you will not bear false witness against him, you will not covet his belongings; if you love your neighbor as yourself, you will not deceive him, you will not trample upon him, you will not seek to take advantage of him, you will not attempt to crush him or to deprive him of his rights and privileges. You will be obeying practically all of the Ten Commandments, if you obey just this one: "Love thy neighbor as thyself." This injunction is the sum total of all the other injunctions of the Scriptures. Love your neighbor as yourself and you will guard against hurting him as you guard yourself against injury.

Man has a three-fold relationship in life, for there are three distinct groups in his circle of contact: He has relatives, friends and neighbors. His emotional attitudes towards each one of these groups are distinct one from the other. He has a natural love for his relatives. Strong ties bind him to them: the same blood flows in his veins as in theirs; he is of the same flesh and bone; the same tissue, the same cells, the same fibres constitute his being. He is inseparably united to them. This union is inherent; it is not consciously brought about; it cannot be destroyed. Parents and children need not have the same interests in life, in order to feel united; they may have different aims, different activities, different ideals, and yet feel very close to each other; their souls, their lives are invisibly cemented, their feelings are knitted together; they are united by the bonds of nature; and love and devotion spring from this union. Therefore is there no injunction in the Scriptures which says: Love thy parents as thyself. Such an injunction would be superfluous, for it is the natural thing to love one's parents. The commandment we have is: "Honor thy parents." For while we love our parents, we do not always honor them; we do not always express our love in terms of reverence and respect; we do not always give them the consideration that is due to them; while we love them, without conscious effort, we do not always regard their admonitions and guidance as applicable to us in our day; we are reminded therefore to respect their judgment, their opinion and their counsel.

Toward our friends, too, the bond is one of love; while the love for our kin, however, is inborn and inherent, friendship is developed. Friendship grows among those who cherish the same ideals, who co-operate for the attainment of the same goal; who respond to the same emotions, who nurture the same thoughts, who carry the same hopes and who have the same outlook upon life. Friendship grows unconsciously; there are invisible attractions, unconscious attachments, intangible fibres that weave two hearts together. In friendship there is a spiritual affinity, which needs no ties of consanguinity to make firm the bond.

There are three ways by which you may recognize a friend. If one is ready to make sacrifices for you, if he does for you what he would do for himself, despite the effort and time and drudgery involved, then he is your friend. If there is one before whom you may speak the truth, the whole truth, without restraint, and without hesitation, and without fear of losing your prestige and your favor, without fear of rebuke or humiliation, then he is indeed your friend. If one co-operates with you in bringing out the highest and the best that is in you, if his presence is stimulating and elevating, if when with him, you feel yourself in a higher, more joyous realm, then he is your friend. What is more natural, then, than to love a friend? What is more natural than to return love for love? The Bible does not enjoin us, nor does it need to, to love our friends. But it tells us: "Love thy neighbor as thyself."

Neighbors—to these we are not related, with these we have not co-operated toward a mutual ideal or a mutual goal, for these we have made no sacrifices, nor have they made any for us. Their past is unknown to us, and their present of no interest, And yet the injunction is to love them "as thyself." The reason is clear. It is the purpose of the Holy Scriptures to generate love where none exists. We are respectful to our neighbors, we use our best manners in their presence, we are courteous to them, but we do

not love them. We are indifferent to them. We
are thrown in their midst, but we do not attempt to be one of them. That is why the Scriptures say: "Love thy neighbor as thyself." Develop a genuine relationship with your neighbor. Your love for your kin is a native one,
your love for your friend is a compensation for
his devotion; but if you give of your love and
devotion to your neighbor, you are giving of
yourself on the basis of human kinship. You
are expressing your love to mankind. You do
not pay, you give; you do not compensate, you
offer—you offer of the finest in you to others.

Love thy neighbor. This does not imply intrusion on your part, nor does it involve un-
called for intimacy, or the delving into his personal matters; it means only a deeply sympathetic attitude towards him. Feel towards him
as you would have him feel towards you. If you
do this, you will not find him overbearing, you
will not find him morose and sour, you will
not find him snobbish and haughty. You will
find that he is a good human being as God
called him here to be.

We do not *have* to have common blood in
order to feel near to each other; we do not

have to have ideals in common in order to be close to each other; we have humanity in common, and this is sufficient ground for love and brotherhood.

Love your neighbor and all coldness and indifference will disappear from your common atmosphere; love your neighbor and you invite hospitality and good will; love your neighbor and you train your heart to its highest powers; love your neighbor and you abolish all hatred and bitterness from the world; love your neighbor and you create for yourself new springs of joy, new sources of happiness.

TOLERANCE

Every race has fostered the ideal of a Messianic era,—an era in which its greatest ambitions would achieve realization and its highest goals be attained. Although the phrase, "Messianic Era," is strictly of Hebrew origin, yet the significance it connotes may well apply to peoples who existed prior even to the Jewish race; for the Messianic epoch is the golden age of every race as perceived by its visionaries and prophets. Each race has had its seers to visualize its perfect future; each race has had its dreams of a Messianic age.

The Messianic ideal, however, differed with each race. To one the conquest of the world, absolute dominion over the other races of the earth was the supreme national ideal. To another, the ascendency of its culture and civilization over the cultures and civilizations of the rest of mankind constituted its vision of a beatific future. To still another, the imposition of its religion upon the rest of the world, the conversion of humanity to its particular form of faith was the ideal to be consummated in a perfect future.

To the prophets of Israel, who gave voice to the ideals of their people, the ideal of supremacy in any form did not appeal at all. To them there was no valid reason why one race should dominate another race, why one nation should subdue another nation, why one culture should trample upon another culture, and why the word of God should be entrusted to one group more than to another. They saw one God and one humanity, one and the same in all its component parts. Therefore the dominion of one element over another element of mankind was to them inconsistent with the Divine plan. The prophet of Israel, therefore, saw a vision of an entirely different nature from those held dear by other races; *his* dream of a Messianic era was that perfect age in which "the wolf shall dwell with the lamb, and the leopard shall lie down with the kid; and the calf and the young lion and the fatling together, and a little child shall lead them." What does this image represent? It represents the ideal of tolerance in this world. The perfect era will be here when the mighty will tolerate the weak, and the weak will no longer fear the mighty; when the powerful will take cognizance and care of the feeble, and these, in turn, will find safety in the presence of the powerful; when the inhabitant of the country will welcome the stranger, and the stranger will find protection and security in every habitation. When all nations, all men, will learn to tolerate and respect one another, the Messianic era will have been attained. This, in ancient days, was Israel's ideal of a perfect future; and it is a universal ideal today.

But while our dreams are turned toward a Messianic era, while our eye is fixed upon the ideal future, let us pause, nevertheless, to contemplate our imperfect present. Let us endeavor to analyze the nature of our intolerance, learn what it truly consists of, where it manifests itself most perniciously, and discover also how we can free ourselves from it.

Intolerance is a harsh and unkind attitude towards those who are markedly different from ourselves. It is a contemptuous disregard for those who are foreign to our beliefs and actions. It is a despotic, abusive aloofness from those whose conduct differs from our own and between whose standards and ours there lie contrasting streams of tradition. Intolerance is dangerous because it marks the beginning of prejudice, which in turn, leads to hatred and bitterness, which, finally, lead to cruelty and destruction.

Intolerance manifests itself in particular instances. It manifests itself against those who foster religious beliefs different from our own, against those who seek material attainments in fields which we ourselves are occupying, and against those whose demeanor, whose actions, whose speech and manners are at variance with ours.

Religious intolerance has been the curse of mankind. From the earliest of days, men, blindly devoted to their own judgments and traditions, have sought to annihilate those who followed traditions or held beliefs different from theirs. Worshippers of one deity sought in its name to ruin the worshippers of another deity. The deities were conceived to be at war one with the other, and their worshippers looked upon themselves as their warriors. And in such struggles, fostered by ignorance and superstition, generations were utterly destroyed, whole nations were completely wiped out of existence. The religious wars, the wars which men fought in the name of their God, were the most cruel, the most disastrous to mankind. Dig into the depths of the world's battlefields, mark the infinite number of prematurely interred bones in their soil, read the history engraved upon them, note that by far the greatest number were the victims of religious war, and you will know the toll that mankind has paid to religious intolerance. Religion in the past was not mankind's source of life, it was rather its ruin. It was not, as it was intended to be, the source of human harmony and happiness; it served instead as the chief cause for dissension and bloodshed. Today while an increased enlightenment and growing civilization have persuaded men of the futility and perniciousness of religious warfare, religious intolerance still has a strong foothold among certain groups and in certain ranks of mankind. Men are still chained by biased tradition, they still harbor the prejudices of the past; they still permit their hearts to be a dwelling place of religious bitterness and animosity. It is for this reason that we must hold fast to the vision of the prophet, to the hope he kindles in us of a better, saner understanding among mankind; a better understanding of God, and through it, a better understanding among ourselves. The time will come when all religious prejudice, all religious intolerance will be obliterated and forgotten. "The wolf shall dwell with the lamb; and the leopard shall lie down with the kid; and the calf and the young lion and the fatling together; and a little child shall lead them." The last phrase "and a little child shall lead them," is extremely significant in the interpretation of this vision. It means that all the combatants, the ferocious and the feeble alike, will cease to strive with one another, and be led by the religion of a child—a religion free from traditional bias, free from bloody prejudices, free from didactic dogmas and stereotyped tenets; free from contempt and disdain for the faith of the other. "And a little child shall lead them," for a child's faith is an innocent faith, and therefore a true faith; a child's faith is a pure faith, it is not alloyed with doubt, it is not mixed with hesitation, it is a faith that trusts God wholeheartedly and whole-mindedly.

We have said also that intolerance manifests itself against those who seek material attainments in fields in which our own struggle for attainment is staged. We are living in a difficult age; strictly speaking, it is the age of individualism. This means simply, each one for himself. Go into the market place and there you will see men striving and toiling with gigantic effort, but each one for himself. Go into the big dwelling places of the city, which many units of humanity inhabit; watch the ways of families who have lived side by side for many years, and you will see that each one lives for and by itself. Observe a man among his social kind; there he may be courteous and friendly, but he carries a cold and reserved atmosphere about him, there is no outpouring of his spirit, of his personality into others; he lives for himself. And the more one lives for himself, the more indifferent does he becomes to others; the more absorbed one becomes in his own self, the more intolerant does he become of those who are at all in his way. We are witnesses to deadly struggles in the world of industry and commerce. We are witnesses to destructive competition and re-

lentless rivalry. We are witnesses to un-
scrupulous methods employed to down and
crush a fellowman. We are witnesses to
merciless and heartless connivances for the
overthrow of a neighbor. Men of this indivi-
dualistic age have failed to form and retain in
their minds a correct image of their relation
to the group. Each one unconsciously regards
himself as the center around which the rest of
mankind sway and swerve. Each one looks
upon himself as the choice of creation, while
the rest of his kind are only to serve him and
make his life more pleasant. Little wonder
then that he pursues with relentless intolerance
that fellowman who is attempting to plant and
reap in the field where he himself has been
making his harvests. Little wonder then that
men are willing to stifle and annihilate those
who venture in enterprises similar to their own.
But they must learn that the center of humanity is not the individual but mankind itself;
that the individual is but a segment, a unit of
the great mass of humanity; that the individual, whether conscious of it or not, is closely
bound to the group by indissoluble bonds, and
that therefore his own happiness can be at-

tained not by contesting with his kind, but by
generating more peace and harmony between
himself and his kind; not by being intolerant
towards those who, like himself, endeavor to
live and prosper, but by being brotherly to
them, by co-operating with them, by extending
a hospitable hand to them. This is the ideal
state of commercial relationship among men,
and this too is expressed in the vision of the
prophet of Israel. The time will come when
"the wolf shall dwell with the lamb, and the
leopard shall lie down with the kid, and the
calf and the young lion and the fatling together, and a little child shall lead them."
The mighty shall dwell in the same field with
the less powerful. The one will not attempt
to devour the other, but shall together nourish
themselves on the substance which God in His
goodness, has provided for them all. "And a
little child shall lead them." Here again this
phrase assumes significance. For the heart of
a young child is untainted with bitterness or
jealousies; it is filled with tenderness and love;
it points the divine way to peace and brother-
liness.

We have said that intolerance expresses itself against those who foster religious beliefs differing from our own; against those who seek material advancement in fields which we ourselves are occupying, and against those whose behavior and demeanor are at variance with ours. This last instance touches upon the problem of social inequality. The earliest records of history show that men have always harbored a strong intolerance for the foreigner, or as the ancient Greeks called him "the barbarian." What is a foreigner? It is one who comes from another land, who speaks a strange tongue, who has a different gait, who uses different gestures, different intonations, and different manners. But while the foreigner may differ much from the native in his exterior, there is no difference at all in his inner life, in the essence of his manhood. They both possess the same heart and the same feelings, they both possess the same aspirations, they both cherish the same hopes and the same God. And yet the tendency is strong even to-day to look down upon the stranger, to limit his incoming numbers, as though God had created the land for one specific group and no other, to be intolerant of his ways and manners, of his distinct way of living and expressing himself. To welcome the stranger is one of the most emphatic injunctions of the Old Testament, to extend hospitality to the foreigner is one of the strongest behests of God. Obedience to this behest will be one of the marks of the Messianic era, and the prophet indicates it in his vision of the perfect future. Clearly he sees the time when men will regard all members of their kind with respect, with forbearance, with tolerance. The time will come when the various elements of humanity will tear down the barriers which rise among them; they will overthrow the false standards which divide their groups and which accentuate their differences, and will instead join in a union of true spiritual democracy and equality, —not only a union of national democracy, but an international one which shall embrace the stranger as well as the sojourner, which shall show partiality to all mankind. "And a little child shall lead them." Once again we find a particular meaning in this figure. For a child is the true democrat. It has come fresh from God, and God does not implant bias towards one and favor towards another. The child, as yet untainted by human standards, is like nature itself, which, also an expression of God's democracy, shows no favor to one more than to the other; its laws are fixed for all. The child has no predisposition to favor one fellow-being above another because of station or position in life. A little child is nearest to God, and from the child therefore we may learn the true ways of God.

The three-fold significance of the prophet's vision, therefore, has it basis in one great ideal—the ideal of tolerance. Intolerance has created too much misery, too much suffering among men. Religious intolerance has stained the earth with human blood; economic intolerance has shattered many minds and broken many lives; social intolerance has humiliated many souls and mortified many spirits. Mankind has followed ways foreign to the way of God, who is loving and tolerant to all His children, who is tolerant even to those who violate His laws, even to those who rebel against Him, even to those who desecrate His holy statutes.

Intolerance is not an inherent divine trait in our nature, and therefore it can be thrown off. Be tolerant and mankind will repay you with tolerance; be tender and kind and loving and mankind will repay you with tenderness and kindness and love; see only the good and the noble and the divine in your fellow-man and only the good and the noble and the divine will express itself through him. We can each individually share in achieving the ideal of tolerance among mankind, and thus individually share in the realization of the great Messianic vision when "the wolf will dwell with the lamb, and the leopard will lie down with the kid, and the calf and the young lion and the fatling together, and a little child will lead them."

LOVE IN MARRIAGE

Marriage is generally looked upon as the culmination of love. We hold, however, that marriage is not the culmination of love, but the beginning of love, not the consummation of an ideal, but the initiative step towards an ideal. And our happiness in marriage depends greatly upon the view-point we take on marriage. If we regard marriage as the realization of an ideal, that is, the materialization of love, it will become to us as a thing which we have already attained and possess. The thing, it is true, is ours, but we lose our zeal, our craving, our warmth for it. The fulfilment of an ideal brings in reality less happiness than the striving for its fulfilment. That which is already ours claims less of our interest, stirs less of our ambition and devotion than that which we still seek to make our own. If marriage denotes absolute acquisition, it is an arid state, wanting the enthusiasm, the joy and the fresh devotion which characterize the quest for the ideal. But marriage, to our mind, is not ac-

quisition, it does not denote absolute possession; it marks rather the incipiency of true
love, the starting point in the direction of the
ideal.

To look upon marriage as the starting point
of love rather than as the fulfilment of love, is
more conducive to happiness in married life.
Two souls will cherish each other more deeply
when they realize that the task of gaining each
other lies before them, not behind them, that
marriage has merely made the way clear, has
given them the opportunity to gain each other,
that new attempts, new efforts, new sacrifices
must be made by both each day to gain more
love, to reach greater depths of devotion, to
realize more and more the ideal of a perfect
union.

Marriage, we are told, is greatly a matter of
chance. By this is implied that the two individuals cannot possibly know each other well
before marriage; they then see each other
through a haze of enchantment, they hear each
other in tones of pleasant music, they interpret
one another in terms of adoration and worship,
they judge each other with utmost tenderness
and even with parental partiality. It is only

after marriage that the spell is broken, the halo removed, and then, two characters, two minds, who have been entirely unknown to one another, meet on the same ground, in the same home, for the purpose of facing life together. The chance in marriage is, then, this: if the two characters are of a similar texture, if the two minds are of a similar training, on a similar plane, and of similar reaction, the chance has been an excellent one for both. If, however, the two minds, at close range, find themselves greatly at variance, thinking on different planes, cherishing different ideals, products of different training and different environments, then each one took an apparently unfavorable chance.

And yet, though marriage is, in a certain respect, a matter of chance, inherently there is no chance of failure in marriage. Two characters may be different, yes; two minds may be of different calibres, yes; they may react in different manner, foster different ideals, follow different ways, and nevertheless they may be harmoniously united and live happily together. Every marriage can be successful, every marriage can be a source

of keen happiness, every marriage can be the
occasion for the expression of deep love, of
abundant tenderness and devotion. Marriage
is strictly speaking a process by which one
personality makes room for another personality. Marital life is essentially a life of mutual hospitality; one heart makes room for
another heart, one mind takes in within its
circumference another mind, one soul invites
another soul into its abode. And through this
mutual hospitality both lives become enhanced,
both hearts become enriched, both personalities gain in depth and in beauty.

In dealing with a personality to whom the
soul has extended its invitation of hospitality,
two elements are essential; one is patience and
the other is tenderness. Patience is essential
in every relationship of life. The ability to
wait is often just as important as the ability
to do and to achieve. The ability to wait until
your irritation passes, until your unpleasant
s t a t e evaporates, until your resentment
vanishes, is a greater quality than that
which seeks forgiveness for embarrassment
which you have already caused, which seeks
to heal a wound that you have yourself in-

flicted, which seeks to pacify a heart which you have dejected and mortified. In patience there is mastery and power; it is by his patience that a man is known. It is with patience as well as with effort that man makes his way in life, that he adjusts himself to his environment, that he builds and creates and advances. What is true in man's adjustment to life outside of the home holds also true to the life within the home. Two characters may be different, two dispositions may be possessed of different reactions, and yet through the exercise of patience these different dispositions will become more and more bent towards one another, they will grow nearer and nearer to each other, until they will in time entirely approach each other without leaving an atmosphere of difference between them. They will then merge into one soul and become one spirit which will act and express itself with a united power and the double strength of the two. Just as impatience in the home only accentuates differences of character, emphasizes differences of disposition and makes two souls grow away from one another, so does patience, on the other hand, bring them nearer and nearer, closer and closer, until their individual pasts are obliterated, their individual traits forgotten; they begin life together with a new life history, with newly moulded reactions, with newly shaped dispositions. Patience simply makes the way for the harmonious qualities in two spirits; it removes all the obstacles on the way to unitedness and peace.

Likewise is tenderness essential in bringing two different spirits to a life of harmony and happiness. Just as patience never fails to clear the way, so does tenderness never fail to gain the heart. Patience alone is not sufficient; patience without tenderness may lapse into a state of indifference, into a state of coldness and stoicism. It is only when patience is linked with tenderness that it becomes a bridge over an ocean of differences. Tenderness has a gaining quality; it makes greater conquests than power and might, it gains more than reason and logic; it is more gracious than precious gifts, it is preferred to wealth and charm. Tenderness is a silent appeal from one heart to another heart, and the appeal is powerful, irresistible, never failing in its end. All differences between two individual souls melt away at the appeal of tenderness. Trainings, dispositions may differ, but hearts do not differ; they are made of the same substance and react to the same emotions, respond to the same appeal. That which softens one heart will also soften another heart. If men and women would keep their best parts for the home, and the rest of themselves for the realm outside the home, they would, perhaps, not be successful in gaining a large circle of friends, but they would never fail to make one strong, devoted life friend. The expression of tenderness in the home must become habitual, it must become constant, it must become more and more intense and whole-hearted.

Thus, patience and tenderness will perpetuate love in the home. Love is a living emotion, and as such it must have freedom, it must have encouragement for growth and expansion. Patience gives it freedom. Tenderness gives it encouragement. Patience overlooks, tenderness forbears; patience minimizes faults, tenderness magnifies virtues; patience stifles anger, subdues bitterness, tenderness urges harmony and peace; patience bridles the tongue, holds back unkind criticism, tenderness adores and encourages. Love is therefore nourished and supported by both.

The chief purpose of marriage is to gain greater happiness. If a man and a woman knew in advance that marriage would bring them only misery, they surely would not marry. Why should they? But life is so arranged that the greatest happiness is attained through love. You are happiest when you have some one that lavishes love upon you, and even more, when you have some one to lavish love upon. If a man and a woman have chosen each other to be the objects of their love, they must also be willing to feed that love, so that it may grow stronger with each day. With the exercise of patience and tenderness, love of itself will grow inseverable bonds.

The human creature possesses a long range of qualities within himself, some of which are the survival of the brute, many others, on the other hand, making for greatness and growth. Those lower tendencies should be discouraged, while the others should be stimulated and animated and inspired. It is easy to bring out the worst in man, and just as easy to encourage the highest in him. Man and woman, in marriage, can easily make each other more bitter, more resentful, more morbid, and they can also make one another more fine, more elevated, more noble. The home must be the center in a man's and a woman's life in which their best is encouraged and their worst discouraged, in which love so fashions them that only the highest in the one is constantly in touch with the highest in the other.

WOMAN'S SPHERE

In the literature of the past, we find reflected two opposite attitudes towards woman. In some of its pages she is exalted to the beauty and sanctity of the angels; in others, she is spurned as the weaker vessel to be trampled upon and broken at will. On the one hand, she is idealized into a super-human creature, and on the other hand she is degraded to a menial and unimportant position in the scheme of things. Literature reflects life even more truly than history; and we find, indeed, that, almost until the present day, woman occupied a most unhappy and cramped position in life; among the higher classes of society, she was spoiled and pampered, weighed down with adulation and flattery; but she was made a creature only of leisure and of play; in the real affairs of life, she was given no role; her voice did not count; it was taken that she had no opinion on matters of real import. She was a gilded bird in a gilded cage; her mind had no room to spread its wings, to exercise itself

in freedom on the vital issues of life. In the
lower strata of society, she was regarded as
little more than a slave or a servant of the
family; a convenient beast of burden, an
animal creature with no spiritual or mental
capacities to place her on a level with man, her
overlord.

The literature of to-day, reflecting the life
of to-day, takes woman's equality with man for
granted, and concerns itself greatly with her
struggles for complete self-expression in her
new freedom, with her difficult choice between
a home and a career. There are few to-day
who would deny woman the right or the ability
to follow a career apart from that of conduct-
ing a home. Too many have done it with
triumphant success to permit of any doubt as
to woman's capacities to stand shoulder to
shoulder with man in almost every field of
endeavor. Yet the fact remains that the woman with a career, highly successful though
she may be, still comes to feel an incomplete-
ness in and a dissatisfaction with her life.
While among those who have taken their place
in the home, there are many, very many, in
increasing numbers, who, after the first thrill

of nesting is over, look with wistful eyes upon their freer sisters, longing to partake more actively in the game of life, to exercise in the market-place the talents and energies to which they give no outlet in the home.

The crux of the problem lies in the fact that the meaning of equality is misunderstood. Equality does not mean identity. Men and women are equal, but they are not identical. There are differences between man and woman which are not arbitrary or temporary, but inherent and permanent. Man and woman must have equal rights, but not necessarily the same functions. Because of inherent, biological and spiritual differences, the equality of man and woman can be built not on the basis of function, but on the basis of their natural qualifications.

God has endowed woman with qualities, or rather reactions, which He denied to man, while, on the other hand, He has given man powers which are more or less distinctly his. In a woman, the emotions are keen and profound; she is gifted with an abundance of tender, sympathetic sentiments, her soul is rich in affection and in kindness. Woman's reaction to a situation is, first of all, that of the heart. A woman feels first, and thinks afterwards; with man a reverse process takes place; he thinks first and then gives way to his feelings. Woman's reaction is emotional, man's logical. And woman's reaction—though it may startle some to hear this—is therefore superior to man's. For the heart knows better than the mind what is right and what is wrong; the heart knows better than the mind what is noble and beautiful and moral and proper. Intuition, the method of the heart, is the short cut to the truth; logic is the laborious way around to the same goal. The mind has this advantage over the impulses of the heart, that it can adjust itself better to environment, that it can quickly select the useful, the practical, the elements that make for convenience and for fortune. But woman, by reason of her special gifts, which are the gifts of the heart, can apply herself to the advancement of the finer calls of civilization.

Of the numerous spheres in which woman may share and lead, there are two, at least, in which she may utilize to the full her God-given powers. The woman who chooses to express herself in these two spheres of achievements, may rightly feel that she is aiding, more than she could in any other way, in the advancement of mankind. I refer to the training of children in the home and the advancement of religion. These are the two most sacred functions in life. They require the consecration of the finer emotions of the human soul; they can bloom only under the care of tenderness and goodness; they require the action of the heart before the speculation of the mind; and therefore I believe that God equipped and qualified woman for these functions.

Our children may receive an abundance of information in school, but their education they can only receive at home. We have said it before, and we cannot emphasize it too strongly, there is a great difference between information and education. Information is the assimilation of facts, the accumulation of knowledge; education is the building of character, it is the transmutation of knowledge into soul substance; it is the extermination of evil influences and the planting of the seeds that make for excellence in the soul of the child. This process needs the vigilant eye and the tender hand of a planter; it is the mother that can best nurture the delicate seedling, and it is therefore her duty as well as her privilege to do it.

I know no one else of whom the child may learn kindness and benevolence. These constitute no part of the school curriculum, and yet it is the most essential part of a child's education. A child does not pick up these virtues on the street; he possesses the potentialities for them, but potential powers must be cultivated, else they remain stunted. It is the mother's duty to bring these soul qualities into action, give them opportunity for expression, watch their growth with zealous eye and tender heart. When you meet men with hardened hearts and closed hands, with greedy desire for wealth and insatiable craving for pleasure, then you may feel assured that some mothers there were who did not perform their duty, who wasted their lives, perhaps, in search of activities out of their natural sphere.

The other sacred sphere that lies open before a woman—the advancement of religion. Our men to-day are so deeply steeped in material tasks that they have actually cultivated a business viewpoint upon everything. Everything is good or bad as it meets the satisfaction or dissatisfaction of business standards. Everything is counted in terms of wealth. It is for this reason, perhaps, that many of our religious institutions are losing their sanctity more and more, and are taking on more and more the air of a conventional or business organization. One who possesses great wealth expects more and is showered with more honors than comes to one of lesser wealth; while those who are poor must content themselves with a back seat, as it were; as though their poverty rendered them inferior to their richer brethren. People are sometimes oblivious to the truth that in the sight of God there are no poor and there are no rich, all are His children and He is the father of them all.

Religion must emanate from the heart; it must express the yearning of profound emotions, it must be a response to a need spiritually expressed. Therefore the masters of the heart are the ones best qualified to become the sustainers of the faith. I am chiefly interested in the Jewish faith, and it is of the Jewish woman, therefore, that I speak. I would like to see the Jewish women in this land realize the great privilege as well as the great responsibility that lies open before them.

Many of our places of worship have conceived the idea of attracting the youth to the synagogue by installing swimming pools and gymnasiums in the temple. No doubt this may draw a number of young people, but it transforms the synagogue into a place of recreation and amusement rather than of devotion. Doubtless if the hall of worship were turned into one of amusement and the Religious School into club rooms, the attendance would be even greater. When bait must be placed in order to entice our youth into the synagogue, we may feel assured that there is something fundamentally wrong in our method of cultivating faith. Faith must not start in the gymnasium; it must begin in the home. The home is the only institution to which manhood can trace its foundation, and religion its devotion; for the mother, the greatest teacher of mankind, dwells in the home.

In Jewish Science, the mother who has the religious upbringing of her children at heart, will find a treasure house to which the key is in her own heart. Through Jewish Science, she may implant the seeds of faith, of health and of happiness in the tenderest years. The lessons of calmness, of cheer, of fearlessness and of trust which she implants in the impressionable years of childhood, will bear still richer fruit in future days; and her children, in the years of their strength and success, will rise up and bless her.

OUR CHILDREN—YOUNG AND GROWN-UP

Children are given to us to keep our emotions warm, to recharge our aspirations, to replenish our hopes, to broaden the scope of our vision, to make us see our earthly immortality. Children are a divine grant, and our very relation to them is divinely determined. Our relation to our children is very much akin to God's relation unto His creation. God's relation to the world is marked primarily by love. He sustains it, He fosters it, He takes care of it, because He loves it. He brings it up from lower to higher states; He leads it from uncouthness unto enlightenment, from dimness unto brightness; He is constantly unfolding it, expanding it, refining it, because He loves it. Similarly is our relation to our children based on love. We rear them, we nurture them, we suffer for them because we love them. We rejoice in their joys, we are unhappy at their woes; we are proud of their success, we are downcast by their failures.

Our heart is surcharged with joy when we watch them take their seats among the prominent of their generation, although they may be leaving us far behind; on the other hand, our hearts bleed, our eyes shed silent tears, if they fail to advance, if they join ranks lower than our own. This is because our hearts are closely tied to theirs, because our spirits are indissolubly united with theirs, because our love makes their happiness more to us than our own.

Because our relation to our children is essentially an emotional one, we are apt to overlook phases in their development which must be primarily controlled by reason. Because of our trembling care for their immediate pleasure, we are prone to encourage in their nature the development of tendencies which may prove an injury to them, and we are apt, on the other hand, to retard or even silence inclinations which would be of great benefit in their later life. We must therefore comprehend fully, first, the stages of their growth, and then, the requirements of each of these stages. Parents must bear in mind three distinct stages in the life of their children.

There is, first, the dependent stage; then, the transitional stage; finally, the independent stage. In each of these stages, they are still naturally our children; but they are different beings in each of these advancing periods. In all these stages they are tied to us with the same blood ties, with the same unseverable bonds, but their relation to the outer world, their adaptation to the environment outside the home, becomes with each succeeding stage, more marked and definite. Also their own individuality, in the process of their growth, becomes stronger and more assertive—seeking constant self-expression.

The first stage, the dependent stage, comprises the early years of the child's existence. At that period, the child is a plastic substance, mouldable and ready to be fashioned; and this is, in a sense, the most important period in the making of the man or the woman. The child is equipped with definite potentialities, with powers which, if properly cultivated and developed, will bring out the best in him and lead him to the highest that may be reached. This is the time when the great man and the noble woman are made. This is the period

when the individual's destiny is greatly determined.   Proper training, proper guidance,
proper encouragement, will bring into play
those qualities which make for greatness and
nobility; on the other hand, erroneous emphasis, faulty development or negligent care
may doom the child to a life of smallness and
failure.

The child, in his dependent stage, when
mother is the only goddess he worships and
father the only great man he admires, must be
trained in at least three things: the performance of duties, the expression of goodness, and
the exercise of faith.   I say the performance
of duties.   The child possesses an abundance
of energy, it is naturally ever-active, but its
action is not always constructively directed.   A
child, no matter how young and how tender,
must be initiated in responsibility.   A child
must have duties and he must perform them
daily and regularly.   These duties may be
small and insignificant; they may consist of
keeping his own toyland in order, of regularly
performing certain tasks; later, of mastering
the knowledge assigned to him, of preparing
lessons without delay.   The stringent perform-

ance of these apparently insignificant duties, prepares them for the performing of the greater duties which, as men and women, life will have in store for them. Children who are trained in punctuality, in effort and in concentration, will, when they mature, find responsibility a pleasure and constructive action a delight; they will be prepared for it from their very early days, and the readiness and effort and concentration that are necessary are instantly at their call. You will observe that I do not say: train your child in wisdom; I say train him in the performance of his duties. For wisdom cannot be transplanted, it is a gift residing within the child itself; it is only when the child is called upon to perform a duty that his natural wisdom will assert itself, his natural intelligence will come into play, and the more obedient he becomes to his tasks, the more deeply does his wisdom center itself upon them.

I said that a child must also be trained in the practice of goodness. There is goodness resident in the heart of the child. God invested the human heart with sympathy, with tenderness and with kindness, but these gifts will remain silent if there is no opening made for their expression, no opportunity given them to assert themselves. A child must be trained in goodness, just as he must be trained in industriousness. He must be initiated in acts of kindness and charity. He must be trained to give away something of his own to one who needs it more than he himself does. He must be trained to forego a pleasure in order to give pleasure to others, he must be trained to speak kind words, think kind thoughts and give expression to kind feelings. You may be assured that he will not lose by it, no one will take advantage of him. And if someone does, the loss will not be on his part, but on the part of the one who does. This world of ours needs benevolence, it needs charity, it needs goodness; man needs a sympathetic attitude from his fellowman, and it is therefore incumbent upon us to bring up a generation that will be able to meet the requirements of humanity. And what is more, those who give free expression to goodness, are themselves rewarded with happiness; when the wholesome elements within our nature are released, they invariably bring to us increasing measures of happiness.

Finally, the child must be trained in faith. Religion is the greatest gift that you may bestow upon your child. By instilling in him a sturdy faith in God, you fortify him strongly against the difficulties and exigencies which life is preparing for him. Strongly entrenched in the knowledge of God's ever-present help, he will not be discouraged by obstacles, nor confounded by difficulties, nor embarrassed by setbacks, nor terrified in the presence of danger. With unflinching faith in God, he will make his way in life, he will preserve his peace and his poise; his heart will always be filled with hope, his mind with optimism; he will refuse to become a prey to disheartening or discouraging influences. Teach the child how to seek God, how to pray. Instruct him in the affirmative method of prayer which Jewish Science teaches. Let him learn today how to invoke God's help, let him turn to God now, and he will continue to do it in his mature days. Do not confuse religion with superstition in the tender mind of the child. Do not appeal to his credulity rather than to his natural desire for faith. Do not impress upon him as religion that which you know his

maturer understanding will outgrow and relin-
quish. But give the child your own God conception, your own religious ideals, your own
prayer, and he will remain faithful to them
all the days of his life.

This training should be given to our children
when they are very young, when they are in
their dependent stage. But there are two more
stages, the transitional stage and the independent stage. In these latter stages, our
children undergo a transformation, and our
attitude toward them must necessarily also
change. In the transitional stage, the youth is
just beginning to see the world for himself.
His individuality is just beginning to assert
itself. His *I* is beginning to act. He is therefore in a rebellious state; he rebels against
dependence. This is a stage in which he begins
to move from the lives of others into his own,
in which he begins to withdraw from the judgments of others into his own, in which he begins to retire from reliance upon others into
self-reliance, in which he begins to discard the
support of others and becomes self-sustaining
and self-supporting. At that stage, we must
still follow our children, still guide them, but

we must keep our distance. Just as they seek their own way, so must we encourage them in it. We must no longer impose our authority on them, for we are their authority no more. We must no longer fondle them with our care, for they are endeavoring to outgrow it and take care of themselves. At that period, we may advise them, but not command them; we may offer them the benefits of our mature experience, but we must not compel them to follow the path which we ourselves have taken. This is an exceedingly precarious period in the life of the child, and yet our judgment must teach us to relax the hold we had upon his younger days. At that period, many things must be overlooked, many things not be heard, many things forgotten; for the spirit of the child is in a rebellious state and he must not be furnished with additional fuel for his rebellious mind. The child is passing from the stage of absolute dependence to the stage of absolute independence, and the bridge between the two stages is extremely narrow; there is room on it only for one. A parent who desires to cross it alongside with him endangers his life; but the faithful parent may walk at a distance behind him, watching for his safety in crossing.

After this dangerous transitional stage, comes finally the stage of absolute independence, the stage in which the children are fully making their own way in life, in which their lives are entirely separate and distinct from those of their parents, in which they have already become a part of the body of mankind. Then even more must the parents forget their authority and their care. Mothers must realize that their daughters have grown up, and fathers that their sons are men like themselves. Then parents must be just friends with their children. At that stage, children *resent* parental authority and dislike parental care. They feel that they are adult, that they can take care of themselves, that they can think for themselves, judge for themselves, feel for themselves; and they consider it an intrusion on the part of anyone, even on the part of a parent, to interfere with the independence of their individuality. At that stage, if parents wish to retain the love and devotion of their children, they must cease to lead, cease to command, cease even to offer voluntary counsel, but should rather delight in the fact that they have brought men and women into the world, who have been able to make themselves independent and are able to take care of themselves. Parents then should be friends, just friends with parental hearts, but no more.

Children are God's gifts. They are given to us, we have said, to enlarge our beings, to train and multiply our sympathies, to increase our emotions, to expand our souls. But parents must watch their children; they must know when to be near them and when to be at a distance; when to give expression to their parental feelings and when to refrain; when to lead them and when to follow them; only then is the parental relation rich and perfect, only then does a mutual blessing rest on parent and child.

HEREDITY

We are well aware of the truth that the present is essentially the offspring of the past. What the world possesses to-day, what mankind has attained to-day, what we are to-day, is due, in large measure, to the efforts, the struggles, the accumulations and deposits of the past. This realization brings to our mind the question as to how much of our being we owe to the past, and how much is our own acquisition; in other words, how much of our actions and reactions is determined by heredity, and how much is the result of our own will.

Many biologists are of the opinion that heredity is the outstanding factor in the life of man, that the parents determine the structure of the individual's body, his stature, the strength of his form, his mental and emotional reactions, the use of his will, his attitude toward life. And to corroborate their opinions, they point to the lives of plants and animals. They point to the great, almost undifferentiated similarity that exists between parents and offspring in the realms of plants, fowls and animals. They point to the Mendelian Law, arrived at through breeding experiments with peas, which showed that the color, size and other characteristics in peas are determined by their heredity. Applying this law to man, they find that it holds true in the color of the eyes and hair and in other visible characteristics. They therefore conclude that man's being is fundamentally determined by heredity. It is needless to say that such an interpretation, were it true, would give us a very pessimistic outlook upon life. We would feel rightly that our whole existence, our manner of thinking, our mode of feeling, our joys and our sorrows, our hopes and our despondencies, our efforts and our creations, as well as our indolence and our failures, all, all were predetermined. Such a conviction would naturally kill our initiative, interfere with our efforts at self-improvement, keep our eyes constantly directed upon the past rather than upon the future, and paralyze progress.

We believe, however, that the influence of heredity has been greatly misunderstood and greatly exaggerated. We find that while man is a product of the past, while heredity contributes much to the making of his self, yet there is a part of his being which only he himself can create. As we examine the law of heredity more minutely, we find that the lower the being the more stringently is it governed by this law, and the higher the being the less does it depend upon heredity for its conduct and self-expression. We can therefore see why those who attempt to draw a close comparison between man and the lower species, such as birds and beasts and plants, must err in their conclusions; for in the lower forms of life, the law of heredity is stringent; the plant shows strictly the character of the plant from which it has been bred; so do the bird and the beast show unmistakably all the characteristics of the generation that sired them; but not so with man. Man, in addition to organic and instinctive reactions, is also possessed of mental and emotional reactions, and in the expression of these higher spheres, he is not dependent upon heredity.

Does this imply that an individual's mind is independent in its quality from the mind of his parents, or that his emotional reactions are different in their nature from those of his progenitors? Our answer is that potentially the difference between parents and children as to mental and emotional powers may be little, but in the actualization of these powers the difference may be great. The mental qualities of a child can usually be traced to its parents, but the manner in which these mental qualities will be expressed, in what sphere they are to be employed, and what they will create, depends entirely, not upon heredity, but upon the training and bringing up of the child, in other words, upon environment. Father and son may both possess the same mental powers, but one may be a manual worker, while the other, with the same native equipment, may become a celebrated artist or a great jurist or an erudite scientist. What may be done with the inherited powers is not predetermined, it is governed by environment and by the individual's own choice. To make this matter of potentiality and actualization more clear, let me use the case of speech as an analogy. Man is born with linguistic organs and powers. Capability for speech is inherent in the human make-up, but what language one shall speak, how many languages he will be able to utilize for the expression of his thought, how clearly and idiomatically he will use his tongue, depend upon conditions after birth. So let us bear in mind that while, potentially, man is bound by heredity, yet in turning his powers into actuality, he is absolutely free; he can utilize them in any way or any manner he chooses, or even not at all.

And just as man has all freedom for the utilization of his mental powers, so has he, and in even greater measure, freedom in the formation of his character. A man's character is not at all determined by heredity. Goodness and meanness, tenderness and coarseness, altruism and selfishness, truthfulness and deceptiveness, are not delivered to posterity through organic transmission. A child is *trained* in kindness, *trained* in altruism, *trained* in truthfulness, or, on the other hand, brought up in selfishness, in rudeness, in deceit. These qualities, good or bad, may be inculcated in the child by his parents, particularly in the early stages of his life, but they are not transmitted to the child by his parents through the power of heredity. Had qualities of character been transmitted from parent to child through heredity channels, there would be little hope of any betterment in these qualities; they would be unchangeable, just as organic life itself is immutable. Character would then be predetermined, and no influence could move or mould it. The fact that character is not inherited, but rather the result of development and training, gives us the greatest hope in the constant progress of human character.

This truth is not new with us; it was indeed well known in the days of old. All the teachings of the Scriptures, all the preachings of the prophets, all the wisdom concerning guidance, inculcated by sage and priest, were solely for the purpose of building and improving character. And our civic and educational institutions to-day are based on the conviction that character is not inherited but capable of being trained and improved, and moreover that the individual himself can train and improve himself. It is for this very reason that our tribunals of justice punish those who commit wrong-doings. It is because mankind recognizes the fact that traits of character are acquired, and that the individual has the power to make his own character, that he is punished for his wrong-doing; for it was done of his own volition.

Just as heredity has little to do with the formation of character, so has it also little to do with the stability of one's nervous state. Too often do we hear one ascribe his or her nervous weakness or other indisposition to a similar state in the parent. One is too prone to believe that because his father or his mother was similarly afflicted, his suffering is due to theirs. How often do we hear: "My mother, too, was a bad sleeper," or, "My father also suffered from indigestion," or, "his father died from cancer." There is no basis for these fears, and experts in physiological science will also attest to that. These ailments are not transmitted through heredity. Children of sickly parents may be strong and healthy, if they are brought up to live a healthy life. Children of nervous parents can have a perfectly strong and vigorous nervous system, if they are brought up to live a serene and optimistic life. It is only if one constantly thinks of and broods over his possible hereditary weaknesses that he is capable of making himself sick and nervous and feeble.

Heredity thus is only the background of life, it transmits too the potential powers that are to be employed in our making. But we have the power to suppress potential weakness in our being, and encourage to expression the potential powers that make for strength, for achievement and for character.

THE SEARCH FOR GOD

We learn from history how prominent a role religion has played in the life of mankind. Religion had exercised its powerful influence upon men of all races, of all ranks, of all stages of historic development, even long before Buddhism and Confucianism and Christianity and Judaism and all the other modern religions had at all come into existence. Religion has been with man always, even in the primordial, prehistoric epochs of human existence. Methods and forms of religious expression have undergone progressive transformation; rituals and prayers and religious ceremonies have been altered again and again in conformity with man's advancing understanding and increased wisdom, but religion as a yearning, as a search, for God, has always been rooted deep in human consciousness. That religion, in its essence, has survived all the stages of human development, and is still to-day the chief source of inspiration and hope for mankind, is unmistakable testimony that there is therein an eternal truth which towers above fancy and superstition, which defies creed and credulity, which transcends knowledge and investigation.

Now, what is this truth in religion that makes it a source of eternal influence? It is simply the realization that there exists an unfathomable Mind whose wisdom transcends all human wisdom and understanding, that there is a Power superior to all human power, that there is a Will infinite in its creativeness and achievement, that there is a Being almighty and omniscient, whom we call God. This realization constitutes the fundamental truth of all religions. Men have differed in their God conception, in their God idea, in their understanding of His essence, in their comprehension of the Divine attributes, in their manner of worship and in their method of prayer; but they have never differed in this: that the God whom they exalt, before whom they prostrate themselves, is possessed of power, of wisdom, of creativeness, superior to their own; else they would not have worshipped Him, they would not have sought His help in their needs and difficulties.

What is it that has given man his God realization, what is it that has given man a belief
in divinity, what is it that has brought to man
the thought of God at all? What is it that has
revealed to man the incomprehensible world
of the spirit? Let me say, first of all, that man
is possessed of an innate craving for God.
Deep in his consciousness there is a yearning
for a Being, supreme and almighty and eternal.
From the unknown regions of his soul there
wells up a longing for an Infinite One, Who
encompasses the vast universe which man himself is unable to comprehend, Who transcends
man's existence as well as the existence of all
that surround him, and Who has it in His
power to help and sustain and restore. This
is what we mean when we speak of God consciousness; it is the spontaneous feeling of
God's presence that rises in man's consciousness. This feeling is particularly active when
man is alone, undisturbed by turmoil and din,
unmolested by anxiety and fear; at such moments, reflective and serene, a keen sense of
the divine presence rises in his consciousness.
This feeling is akin to all the other innate human feelings; it is like love, like sympathy,

like hope—feelings which have been placed in man in the very formation of his being. This feeling of the divine presence is man's chief clue to God's existence. One really needs no proof—though that too is not wanting—in order to become convinced of the existence of God; man believes in God because he is possessed of an inherent tendency to believe. Faith is inborn and natural; the abnormal and foreign thing to our nature is unbelief. One who cherishes faith, lives, therefore, a perfectly harmonious life; he suffers no inner perturbance, no soul disruption, no spiritual disquietude, he is not beset by perplexing question marks on every hand. God to him is not a puzzle, not a question, God is to him an answer, a solution to all the puzzles and uncertainties which he encounters in nature and in his own life. It is the man who lives without faith that finds himself constantly entangled in the meshes of life, constantly perplexed, constantly in doubt as to the value and meaning of existence. The lack of faith is akin to the lack of any other vital qualities in man; the lack of faith is as undermining as the lack of hope, or the lack of sympathy, or the lack of love, all of which are essential to a full and harmonious life. In the normal man, all these are present, and faith is one of the attributes of the normal mind.

But man believes in God not only because he senses instinctively the Divine Presence, but also because he arrives at the truth of divine reality through his logical reasoning. When man finds himself in the presence of the great works of nature, his soul is captured by an overmastering conviction of the presence of a great Creator. While his heart is filled with admiration and awe before these eternal masterworks, his mind unfailingly connects them with a master worker who called them into existence. One cannot stand before the overwhelming power and beauty of the sun, or gaze upon the quiet, perpetual light of the moon and stars, or look up the unfathomable seas, and say, with reason, unto himself, "all these have no creator; they have created themselves." One cannot meditate upon the beauty of field and flower, upon the blooming tree and the giant rock, upon the limpid stream and verdant valley and say unto himself that all these were their own makers, the designers of their own forms, the projectors of their own functions, the generators of their own energy, the determiners of their own seasons and of the length of their existence. Logically, one cannot but arrive at the truth that there is an Eternal Designer, an Infinite Creator, an Everlasting Sustainer from whom all existence and all reality emanate, one who is the Designer and Creator and Determiner of all.

We do not, when we say this, disregard in any way the investigations and speculations of the human mind concerning the growth and progress of existence, we do not depreciate the teachings of the theory of evolution; but this theory is not, nor does it claim to be, a theory of existence and of life, but rather a theory of growth and progress. It does not attempt to teach how existence came to be, nor does it attempt to show what power, other than the Supreme Power, impels the world in an onward direction. Evolution explains how forms, organisms, creatures, have evolved from the simple to the complex, from the lower to the higher, from the non-intelligent to the intelligent, but the evolutionary theory does not at all explain how any of these beings have come into existence, nor does it point to any tangible, comprehensible force that is responsible for the progressive movements of reality. Evolution therefore is merely a theory which expounds how nature has developed; but it is no more than that, nor does it claim to be more.   When one searches for the ultimate cause of existence, when he earnestly seeks for the source of all energy and power, for the originator of all, for the designer of all, for the guide and determiner of all, he must find —God.

Not only by steeping oneself in nature, but also by reflecting upon one's own being, may one come to the realization of God.   One may find his Creator, when he pauses to analyze the complete nature of his own being and asks himself: whence this existence, this life of mine?   Who is it that furnished me with limbs and organs and functions?   Who is it that supplied me with thought and feeling and effort that I may be able to maintain myself while on earth?   Who is it that recharges my energies, that gives power and sensitivity to my faculties and senses that I may be able to fit and adjust myself to my environment?

Man may find his God when he reflects further upon the transiency of his being; when he realizes that his body is here for but a limited number of years, that his knowledge is insignificant compared with the endless mysteries that surround him, that he is in the true sense of the word neither lord of the land, nor master of the air nor ruler of the elements, but that, on the contrary, he is subject to the mood and passion and eruption of these vast embracing forces in which he finds himself, he will then unfailingly come to the conviction that there must exist One Who is the true ruler, the true master, the true owner of the land and of the air and of the elements and of all existence, One who is the true owner of man's life, the true Creator of man's energies, who is the true master of man's years, under whose Providence man lives and maintains himself.

Man thus realizes God's presence both instinctively and rationally, both through his deeper emotions and through earnest reflection. Man's higher nature leads him to higher truths, man's profounder self yearns to identify itself with God. This is what we mean by true religion.   It is the craving of a heart to identify itself with the greatest of all realities, it is the yearning of a soul seeking to soar to the sublime source of its being, it is the earnest endeavor of a mind to commune with its Maker, it is man's realization that he lives with and has his being in God.

RELIGION IN THE MARKET PLACE

Perfect harmony, both with oneself and with outer circumstances, is the smoothest road that man may take to happiness and success. When inner and outer harmony blend to produce unity in the soul, then man reaches a godlike mood, and his powers of achievement become godlike.

By inner harmony we mean, first of all, a state in which all the powers with which a man is endowed, co-ordinate and co-operate with one another; where there is, for instance, no conflict between the mind and the heart, between thought and emotion, between desire and discretion; where there is no war between conscience and ambition; where the will does not become rebellious to the judgment. Such inner harmony brings about that blessed mood which we term peace of mind.

Outer harmony means first of all peace between a man and his environment, between himself and his fellow-men, and, more important still for his happiness, between himself and his work. Harmony between a man and his neighbors brings a man inner joy; by cherishing love for them, he unconsciously receives love from them in return. Likewise, when there is harmony between him and his interests, he experiences an inner joy; and this joy stimulates him to greater efforts which multiply his rewards.

A man's work, therefore, must be of such a nature that his attitude towards it is one of love. No matter what other considerations are involved, he must devote his days and his years to it first of all because he loves it. Only then will he be able to inject his whole power into it, and derive the full benefits from it. Man's work must first of all be a haven for his overflowing energies, it must be a school for the training of his faculties, it must be a fertile field in which his mind may grow, it must be one of the chief sources of his happiness. All of this is true when a man loves his work. If, on the other hand, there is no harmony between him and his tasks, if he has a distaste for them or even indifference, if he does not earnestly love his work, then he will never be happy with it, no matter what material profits may accrue. In such work, his mind does not achieve its finest growth, nor his faculties their highest development. Such work may pull, overpower, hustle and rush him, but he himself does not develop; his profits may grow, but he himself does not, because there is no harmony between himself and his work.

When a man is in harmony with his work, he never tires of it. He does not count the hours; he does not brood upon the past, he keeps his gaze upon the future. His thoughts are not centered on the amount he has already achieved, but on the task that is yet to be done. The artist never tires of his work; and the artist is the hardest of workers. To practice one passage or one phrase for hour upon hour until perfection is attained is not an uncommon thing among artists. I know of one who, after having worked steadily all day and late into the night, on being reminded of the lateness of the hour, smashed the time-piece on which the hour had been shown him, and cried triumphantly: "Now I can go on, time no longer exists for me," and continued his work till the morning. You have heard of poets who write and rewrite one line as many as a hundred times. You know of scientists who, day after day, are content to be cooped up in their laboratories, and tied to their microscope, delving deeper and deeper into the mysteries of nature. These men never tire. Their strength and their courage renews itself in their work. They are happiest when they are at their task, and unhappy when kept away from it. The secret of their gigantic energies lies in the harmony between themselves and their work. They love their work, and one never tires of that which he loves.

In contrast to this, take the man who is engaged in an occupation which does not interest him, which he undertakes only because of the remuneration connected with it. Without love for his work, he tires quickly, he counts the clock-ticks, becomes impatient with the slowness of the hours, and feels relieved when his day's work is at an end. His whole attitude is the reverse of the one in which there is harmony between man and his work.

Work is not the misfortune that some of us regard it to be. It is a divine privilege, and the work, no matter what it is, with which we find ourselves in harmony, creates within us a joy such as no other phase of existence can produce. Work is divine in origin. God himself works. The creation and maintenance of the universe implies never-ceasing work. And therefore creative achievement by man also necessitates arduous and incessant work. We strengthen the harmony between ourselves and our work, when we look upon it, as we should look upon ourselves, as divine in origin. We must impregnate our tasks with a spiritual and religious viewpoint. It is a grave error to draw a line of demarcation between the sacred and the secular. We are accustomed to consider our stay in the House of Worship as sacred, and our stay in the market place as secular; our utterances in the synagogue as sacred and our speech in the street as secular; our attitude, our reactions at the Shrine as sacred, our attitude and reactions in our business as secular. Such a division is arbitrary. It is man who has drawn this line of demarcation. God never intended life to be so. There is no reason why a man's work should not be a tribute to God, as well as his prayer. Work, too, is a form of prayer, for it expresses the fulfilment of a divine instinct. There is no reason why man should not have this religious attitude towards his work or his business. It is a custom to feel religiously in the House of Worship; but the House of Worship is not the only place wherein God dwells. The whole Universe is God's abode, and whatever man does, he does it before God. Everything is sacred, everything is divine. In olden days, the Jew was wont to build his synagogue, not near his home, but in his market place, as a symbol that there is no division between religion and business, as a reminder that one cannot be religious in the synagogue and impious when away from it, as a reminder that he is standing always before God.

By divorcing religion from business, we are doing ourselves an irreparable injury. We expose ourselves to the dangers and traps that business has in store for us. The dangers and traps of business are the anxiety, the worry, the fear which follow its trail. Every new investment, every new undertaking is apt to be followed by tremors of fear, vexation of spirit, sleepless nights and restless days. Religion removes these foes from business. The reason that the business man is so pursued by the anxieties of his own imaginings is because he conducts his business single-handed. If he felt that, no matter what the outcome of the enterprise might be, someone was always backing him, he would never be depressed in the anticipation of the results. If he were assured, for instance, that his banker was always behind him regardless of the consequences of his undertaking, his fears and anxieties would vanish. He who injects a religious attitude into his business has this assurance of support constantly behind him. Just as the Psalmist did in days of old, so he too finds in God a tower of strength, a sustainer and protector in the present, and a haven for the future. "God is my light," says the poet. "God is my guide and my help." "God is my shepherd." These are not merely poetic exclamations, they are the veritable experiences of the man who trusts in God. What the Psalmist experienced in days of old, we may unfailingly experience to-day. Trust God at least as you would trust your banker, confide in Him as you do in your best friend, pray to Him as you would petition a man for help, know that you have in Him a staunch and unfailing partner, and by so doing, you will remove fear and worry from your enterprises.

There are too many tragedies in the life of men of affairs.   There are too many breakdowns, too many nervous prostrations, among men of enterprise.   Too often we find this the result of business life without faith.   Whatever you do, remember that God is at your right hand to guide you; whatever new plan you may conceive, pray first for help before you make ready to translate it into reality. Let your first thoughts be of the Great Invisible Partner, who is ever ready to help you. And do you but call upon His help.

HEALING THROUGH JUDAISM

Judaism is essentially a practical religion. Study the Old Testament carefully and you will see that it contains a code of laws for application to daily life. It takes into consideration human frailties as well as human potencies; it examines man's tendencies to virtue and his temptations to wrongdoing, and then seeks to encourage his virtuous nature and bar the road to evil. Judaism is a practical religion, because it lays down concrete laws of demeanor, showing man how to conduct himself in every relation of life. There is no superstition or irrational theory of life in the Old Testament. There is no theory of salvation, nor an exposition of the life hereafter. Every law, every injunction refers to man's conduct in this tangible, comprehensible, convincing world.

Being the religion of daily life, Judaism also offers man laws of health and healing. And it treats of the two aspects of healing, first, of preventive measures, and second, of curative applications. Medical science today is endeavoring more and more to develop and perfect preventive medicine; hence it is laboring on many tests for the prevention of the more perilous diseases. The child of today is given inoculations and injections to fortify him against the ravages of the so-called diseases of childhood. Similarly, measures both of prevention and cure are laid down in the Sacred Scriptures. Preventive measures are indicated in the Mosaic Laws; curative methods were practiced by the prophets, and especially by the Psalmist. The Mosaic Law insists on stringent cleanliness, on the use of uncontaminated, unadulterated food, on the use of clean water, on personal cleanliness and purity, on the application of sanitation in every place and in every environment. The dietary laws have, in fact, no other purpose than that of preventing disease. Eat not the flesh of the swine, for the swine is an unclean animal; it is fed on unclean food, and is therefore the carrier of disease. Abstain from eating the flesh of the wild beasts and the rapacious fowls, for there are poisonous substances in their composition, and these injurious elements, entering your body, may breed disease. Abstain from consuming the blood of animals, for the blood is often charged with impurities, and these may become transfused into your blood, there to generate disease. Do not touch an unclean object, for uncleanliness is the origin of disease. Be sure to wash your body and particularly your hands as often as possible. All these injunctions, laid down in the Bible and in the Talmud with scrupulous rigidity, have no other object than that of preventing disease.

Where ailment has already made its entrance the prophets point the way to relief. Help must be sought from God. As God is the source of life, as He is the spring of existence, as He is the very fountain of health, so is He the One to be invoked for the restoration of that which has been impaired. That which man himself creates, man himself can restore. If a piece of machinery or mechanism, built by human hand, ceases to function properly, it needs but a human hand to restore it to efficiency. But man himself is the creation of God, and if, therefore, a human function or organ is impaired, it is not man but God who is able to restore it.

The creation of man is analogous to the creation of the world. God unfolded this world from a formless nebula; He built it from apparently insignificant substances. He rolled out the planets from immaterial vapors, He constructed the sun of trivial substances. But all these He invested with power from His own inexhaustible Fountain of power, with energy from His own infinite storehouse of energy, and with His own wisdom and direction. This very same process He employed in the creating of man. From an insignificant cell does God form man; out of trivial substances does He build his bones and knit his veins, and weave his skin; but in this substance He has stored Wisdom and Intelligence, pouring it fourth from His own infinite Wisdom; He has endowed man with Health and Vigor, out of His own infinite storehouse of strength and power. When man, through ignorance or wilfulness, becomes ill, it is for him to turn to his Builder, to his Creator, for restoration. And this he may do through prayer. The prophets and sages therefore propose prayer as the curative, as the restorative measure. Offer prayer to Him who has built you and He will restore you to health, for He is good and merciful, He seeks the happiness of those whom He called into existence. Seek His help earnestly, wholeheartedly, and your prayer will be answered, your health and strength will be restored.

The Mosaic Law, we see, emphasizes, preventive measures, and the prophets and Psalmist show us how to regain our health when it has become impaired.

In Jewish Science, too, we accentuate the two aspects of healing, the preventive and the curative. But in Jewish Science we go one step further in our search for the causes of ailment. In the Old Testament, the causes of illness were found to be mainly of physical origin, and therefore the dietary laws and the laws of sanitation were strongly impressed upon the people; in addition to physical sources of disease, we learn, in Jewish Science, that ailment may also have its origin in the mind. Worry is as fertile a cause of sickness as contaminated water and adulterated food. Fear and anger are as likely to bring on disease as uncleanliness and impurity. We therefore, in Jewish Science, eliminate from our lives these mental obstacles; for we know that, just as an unclean body is one of the direct causes of disease, so too is an unclean mind. The mind like the body must be cleansed of unwholesomeness and impurities.

In Jewish Science, we follow the method of the prophets and the Psalmist in our restorative methods; we seek help from God, the Giver of life and health, the Sustainer of all. But here, too, we make one addition in the method of invocation. While many of the prophets and sages still beheld God as seated on a lofty throne, and to this High Throne they addressed their prayer for help, we find that prayer is even more efficacious when it is offered to the Divine Mind in man. The same God that dwells in heaven also fills the earth with His Presence; the same Divinity dwells in the star and also makes His abode in man. Man is a shrine for God, just as heaven itself is. In our prayer for help, therefore, we pray to the God in us; we say: "The God consciousness in us expresses itself in health." And this form of prayer is more readily answered, because when we offer a prayer to the Divine Mind within us, we offer it with the consciousness of His nearness, with the realization of

His immediate presence; our prayer is then offered earnestly and devoutly, and such prayers are always answered.

Judaism, thus, is the religion of life. Its laws, its commandments, exist for the purpose of guiding and directing and preserving man. Judaism, through its various stages of development, ancient as well as modern, has evolved definite ways and measures by which man may save himself from the attacks of disease and suffering. Cleanliness of body and mind, purity and optimism will prevent disease; scientific prayer and earnest devotion will heal disease, if it has already found lodgment. Prayer will restore to health and strength, for the Giver of life is also the supplier of strength, the Sustainer of all.

WHAT IS MAN?

We can observe man from two view-points. First, from the view-point of man's own world; that is, the world which he himself builds and plans and creates, the world which he himself has cultivated and developed, which he has improved and advanced with his intellect and energy. Here we find man powerful and dominant, heroic and masterful. Here, in his world, he has conquered the beast and the brute; he has changed the face of the earth to satisfy his needs and his tastes; he has built cities and united continents and explored the ends of the earth. Here, in his own world, he is delving and searching; he is soaring among the clouds and diving into the very depths of the sea. Here he is forming philosophies and scientific systems, and he is rising and advancing in his various enterprises. Here he is indeed a master and a creator.

We can, however, behold man from another angle: from the viewpoint of the universe, from his relation to existence at large. Here you find man a very insignificant creature. Compare him to the immeasurable stars, and you will find him infinitesimal. Compare his strength with the strength of the rock, of the mountain, and you will find him feeble. Compare his will to the will of the stream, running its unceasing course, or to the violent wind, tearing away all that is in its path, and you will find it faint and sluggish. Compare man's conscious wisdom to the wisdom that rules the world; compare man's wisdom with the wisdom that set the planets into space and formed harmony and order among them; compare man's creative power with the power that created all reality, and you will find man hopelessly wanting and failing. Compare man's span of life with the infinite ages of the universal bodies, which man daily observes, and you will find his existence fleeting and transient. From this second view-point, then, man is but a moving, stirring particle in an infinite ocean of reality.

Reflecting upon man from these two viewpoints, one is prompted to ask, with the Psalmist: "What is man?" Is he a major creation of God, or an insignificant and fleeting atom of the universe? Is he here to have dominion over the earth, or is he a mere plaything in the hands of the elements?

Before we attempt to answer this question, let us pause to consider, for a moment, the composition and nature of man. We are told that man is composed of at least seventeen chemical elements—elements which are not unique in the composition of man, but which are present everywhere in nature. Man's body is made up of cells, common to all creatures, but specifically arranged to form the human frame. Then, man is possessed of the breath of life; but this too, as we know, is not the special gift of man; every self-moving thing in the universe is filled with life. Man is endowed with senses; he can see, hear, taste, smell and touch. With his senses, man comes in touch with his environment. His senses are the doors and windows through which the outer world enters into his being. But senses, too, are not unique to man; all the forms of the higher order of beings possess them. According to the Scriptures, man was the last creature called into creation, and according to modern sciences, too, man is the survival of countless generations of species that preceded him. In other words, all the elements of nature joined their substances to form man's body, endless generations of species contributed to his life and senses, so that man might stand at the height of creation. But wherein lies man's distinction from the rest of the creatures of nature?

We say that man's distinction lies in his freedom. It was God's design to form a free being and He formed man. All the actions of all other things and beings in existence are determined by their instincts and not by their will. They have not the freedom to choose their own course and select their own goal, or determine their own future. Man alone can. The stream *must* run a downward course, it cannot flow upward; the tree must flower in its season, it cannot alter its time; the star must race in its orbit, it has no choice of its own; the animal, wild or domestic, the beast, the fowl, all must follow the routine of their instincts and cannot deviate from their rule. But man can do as he please. He can change his course, he can alter his goal, he can deviate from the paths of the past, he can build his own world, determine his own destiny. Man is free. He can make progress or regress, he may advance or deteriorate, he may bring great good to mankind and to himself, or he may be the cause of injury and evil.

But when man uses his freedom for advancement and progress, he gains; when he uses his freedom for destruction, he loses. For advancement and achievement man is compensated with happiness; when he chooses regress and deterioration, he accepts at the same time unhappiness. Man is given freedom chiefly in order to enable him to become a master—a master over circumstances and a master of himself. Man with his powers and his freedom of action, must never complain of the circumstances in which he may find himself, he must never complain of his destiny, he must never moan his lack of opportunities. He is free; he can change his circumstances, he can change his destiny, he can create his opportunities. Things do not come to those who can walk; they must go and obtain them. Things do not grow of themselves for those who can plow and sow; they must be planted, and tended and watched with care. Caves are not meant to shelter those who can build structures for habitation. The primal forest is not the dwelling place for those who can advance civilization. In other words, while, for the lower order of beings, God has prepared things, as it were, ready-made, He has given man his materials in the rough, that he may exercise his freedom in fashioning them to his purpose. Therefore man need never submerge himself, or resign himself, to apparently unfavorable circumstances. He must keep his head high above them. He must conquer them, mould them, fashion them, until they conform to his will for good.

And just as freedom was given to man to enable him to master his circumstances, so was it given to him also to enable him to master himself. There may be in a man's make-up unwholesome tendencies and desires; he may be possessed of injurious habits and noxious reactions, which are detrimental to himself and to others; but he must never say: "I cannot help it, it is a part of me." Of course, it may be a part of him, but that is the very part he must and can change. Let him keep back his temper, let him not say it is a part of himself. He can annihilate it, he can uproot it, he can stamp it out of existence. He can refuse to lend himself as a tool for its violence and destructiveness. For that purpose he was given freedom. Let him not say: "I am of a jealous disposition, but I cannot help it, it is a part of me." Of course he can help it. He can face it and discover its pretences and its false-hoods, he can unravel its deceitfulness and its suspicions, he can unmask it and free himself from its hold. For that purpose he was given freedom. Let him not say: "I am full of fears, I know that I should not fear, but I cannot help it, it is a part of my being." Let me tell him that fear is not a part of his being; God did not intend him to be fearful, he can drive his fear out of existence. He can analyze it, he can persist against it, he can affirm against it, he can discourage it until it leaves him; for in the presence of an inhospitable at-mosphere, fear will refuse to stay. Man can drive out fear. For that purpose he was given freedom.

Man's freedom was given to him for pro-gress: that he might master his circumstances and himself. We are told that man comes from a low origin, that his ancestry may be traced to the ape and the brute, that he comes from a stock common to all the lower forms of existence. Be it so. More credit to him. It shows that he has used his freedom in a progressive direction. He has stripped himself of the brute, he has freed himself of the ape, he has passed and left behind him all the generations and ages of savagery and barbarism, he has made a man of himself. What his progress was in the past, it must be, in a still further direction, in the future. Man must utilize his powers and his freedom in battle against his circumstances and himself, until he attains perfection.

What is man? Man is greater than the stars, for he is free to direct his course, which they are not. He is greater than the elements, for he can choose his own direction; he is greater than all the forces of nature, for he is not directed, he directs himself. What is man? Man is a free being.

GOOD AND EVIL

From days immemorial, the human mind has been delving into the problem of evil. In fact, so much so that the good has been frequently overlooked. The question that has troubled mankind has been: Why does evil exist? And evil has been defined as error, sin and suffering. Why, first, does error exist? Why does truth hide itself, why does it not present itself at first sight? Why need man undergo the trials of error before he comes to the realization of truth? Why is there so much error in the nature of the comprehension of existence? Why so much error in man's adjustment to his environment? Why so much error in man's relation to his neighbor?

Again, why is there sin in this world? Why does man go astray? Why does he commit acts against which his better judgment protests, which conscience vehemently condemns? Why does man harbor sinful thoughts that vitiate his mind? Why does he choose sinful ways which his better self rejects? Why does he act in violation of the law of God and contrary to the higher standards of men?

Finally, why does suffering exist? Why does so much misery, so much pain, so much grief, so much illness darken this world. In short, again, why does evil exist? Would it not have been an infinitely more ideal state for man if there were no error, if there were no sin and if there were no suffering.

Our answer to the question, why does evil exist, is that evil is not a fundamental element in nature. There is no evil in nature. Nature is essentially perfect. God is good, and the laws of God in nature are uniformly good. Search for the outcome of each cause, follow the aim of each phenomenon, trace each process to its goal, and you will find that all these are here for the purpose of advancing life, of augmenting beauty, of creating deeper and still deeper harmony in the world. Nature is pure, there is no sin in nature; nature is clear-sighted, there is no error in nature; nature is vigorous and powerful, there is no weakness in nature. There is therefore no evil in nature.

We cannot, as we see, speak of evil in nature, we can only refer to it as existing in the life of man. We have often said, however, that man is a part of nature, that he is, moreover, a creation of God, just as nature itself is; how then does it come about that he possesses in his make-up imperfections from which nature itself is free? It is indeed true that man is an integral part of nature; in fact, it is the only way by which we can account for the existence of man; but man possesses one distinct attribute of his own—a quality which is the special gift of man. This is the power of volition, or the power of choice. Nature cannot choose, it does not need to choose. Nature never finds itself at the crossroads, nature is never beset by doubts, nature is never perplexed; the road which nature travels is always illumined and clear; its progress is not obstructed, its advance is not impeded; it follows directly the laws of God which lead to perfection.

This is not the case with man. As a part of nature, man too is possessed of all the elements that make for perfection, but while nature at large has no choice, it *must* travel on the highway to perfection, man has the power of choosing; if he so desires, he too may make perfection his goal, but if he does not desire it, there is nothing to compel his advance in that direction. There is no inherent force in him, as there is in nature, to *compel* his compliance with the law of God that makes for goodness and perfection. Here we can see where evil would make its way and claim existence. When man refuses to force himself into the way of good, when he does not consciously identify himself with the highest, the best and the highest will not force themselves upon him, and in the consequent absence of these, there is suffering, sin and error.

That phase of evil termed suffering is surely not inherent in man's make-up. It is not true that man is born to endure pain and illness, to be the butt of misery and unhappiness. We say in Jewish Science that man is called into existence to be vigorous and healthy, to rejoice and be happy all the days of his life. Sickness is not God's creation, it is man's choice; misery is not God's decree, it is man's own acquisition; sin is not an allotment of God, it is the option of man.

You may ask, how can it be that sickness and suffering are man's own selection? Who

would willingly choose to afflict himself? Who
is there that is seeking sickness or loves pain
or prefers misery to joy? No, directly no man
chooses suffering, but indirectly he does. Sickness, pain, suffering are the consequences of
the wrong choices which man makes. When
a man selects an erroneous method of living,
or an imperfect manner of conduct, he is usually not aware of the wrong he commits against
himself, he does not at the time of his erroneous choice realize that together with such a
choice he also chooses misery and sickness and
pain. If pain came before, not after, the com-
mission of a wrong act or preceded the initia-
tion of a faulty habit or harmful routine, then
mankind would have been absolutely perfect;
for pain would then prevent man from choosing
evil. But suffering comes usually as a consequence, and man must therefore *learn,*
through his own experience or through the experience of those that precede him, how to
avoid that which leads to suffering. He must
learn to recognize the ways of perfection and
follow them.

Which are the perfect ways that man must
follow? We say, in Jewish Science, that the

perfect ways of God may be seen clearest in
nature. Let man choose to follow the method
of nature, and evil will cease to be, or rather,
it will never come into existence. Observe
that there is poise in nature. There is no
hurry, no excitement in nature. The flower
works for the attainment of maturity, the tree
strives for its fruition, the stream seeks to
plough for itself a deeper bed, the field labors
for more abundance, the landscape for more
beauty, and yet all these attain their goal with
serenity and with ease. All these, in their
process of growth, expend energy and take in
energy. But nature is never in debt, it never
expends more energy than it takes into its
veins and arteries. There is a perfect balance
between assets and liabilities in the strength
of nature, and therefore nature's strength is
never sapped, it continues its advance with
ever overwhelming power. Man loses his natural strength, and becomes ill, when he deviates from his natural poise, when his growth
or his gain are attained through processes contrary to those of nature. When a man thinks
that joy can be attained only through excitement, and gain only through intensity and

rush, and lets this atmosphere of excitement
permeate his whole world and his whole life,
he is then violating the divine law of poise and
tranquility, and in consequence of this erroneous process, falls ill and becomes subject to
suffering and unhappiness.

Again observe nature. The course of nature
is always directed towards the higher goal.
In order to rise, nature undergoes definite
changes. It casts off its lower forms and takes
on a higher one; it never retrogresses, it never
looks backward, but always moves forward to
attain greater heights, to achieve greater perfection. It evolves from the lower to the higher, from the inorganic to the organic, from
ignorance to intelligence; and with each advance it makes, it casts off the previous lower
state. But it holds the gains it makes, it retains
its acquisitions. Man, too, must always make
efforts to rise to higher heights, and at the
same time hold on tenaciously to the moral
and spiritual possessions already attained.
Through this process, man will gradually find
himself removed further and further from
error and sin. The spiritual acquisitions of the
past must be strongly guarded, the moral vic-

tories which one gains himself must not be allowed to slip back. These must be strongly fortified, unceasingly exercised and practiced. Man himself has created evil, and man himself can free himself from it.

CHARACTER

It is our belief that there is one attribute, and only one, that determines man's position among his fellow men, and that is *character*. A man of high character stands out among his kind, he radiates his essence upon his fellowmen. A man of character can touch every heart with the power of *his* heart, he can influence every mind with the fineness of *his* mind; his every act, his every word, bespeak, unconsciously to him, the nobility of his soul.

What, let us consider, *is* character? Character originally meant the stamp of a thing, an impression placed on an article in order to distinguish it from the rest of its kind. When this term was transferred to describe man, it retained its original meaning. Character has come to designate that phase in man's being by which he is distinguished among his kind. Character, however, has little to do with the mental qualities of the individual; it is not dependent upon the depth of one's mind, nor upon his artistic tastes, nor upon the keenness of his sense perceptions or the clearness of his vision or the quality and color of his imagination. Character is a resumé of the qualities of the human heart; it has chiefly to do with the relationship between man and his fellow men, it is the touchstone of the harmony between the individual and the group.

Let me state at the outset that character is not an inherited possession. The fact that we often find strong resemblances of character between a child and one or both of its parents, does not contradict this assertion. Children will resemble their parents in character, not because they have received character predispositions, through the channels of heredity, but because they strongly imitate, consciously or unconsciously, for the most part unconsciously, the reactions, the manners, the attitudes of those who rear them and are devoted to them from the very early days of life. If a child were reared in a strange environment, away from its parents, its character reactions would be entirely different from those of its parents; for the qualities of character are acquired and not inherited.

Now, if character is not inherited, how is it

acquired? Character can best be conceived as an invisible structure which one builds for himself throughout his life. Some of these structures attain towering altitudes, some reach only mediocre heights; some are strong and beautiful, filling the heart of the beholder with pleasure, some are frail or ugly, and repellent to human refinement. But the building of a great character is not a complex matter. Since character is the keynote of the relation between the individual and his fellow beings, good character is nothing more than the habit of being thoughtful of other human beings. Every one unconsciously expects consideration from others; every man, in time of need, expects help from others; for his achievements, every man expects appreciation and respect from others; in his daily dealings and transactions, he expects truthfulness and uprightness from others; in his social affiliations, he expects kindliness and good breeding; from his neighbor, he expects friendliness and courtesy, from his friends he expects devotion and self-sacrifice. Now, if a man trains himself into the habit of giving to others all these things which he expects from them, if he compels himself to give to others consideration proportionate to the consideration he expects from them; if he judges them as he would expect them to judge him, if he co-operates with them and helps them and respects them and is sincere and honest with them, as he would wish them to be with him, he is building for himself a good character. That is what Hillel Hanasi, the celebrated Jewish sage, intended when he said, "That which is objectionable to yourself, do not do unto others." And although it is a simple instruction, it is not an easy task to accomplish; for we must first battle with hampering and opposing tendencies, we must struggle against self-centredness, we must suppress and annihilate greedy, grasping desires, we must banish selfishness, and only when we have conquered all these ugly tendencies within us, can we become as thoughful of others as we expect them to be of us.

But there is a still higher terrace in the structure of character which we may build for ourselves. One has attained the highest reaches when he has schooled himself to be *more* thoughtful of others than he expects them to be of him. Such a one keeps his own self always

in the rear; he is ready and happy to give, to
make sacrifices for others, while for himself he
expects little or nothing from others. He looks
upon his own needs as insignificant, he is happier in self-denial than in acquisition, and
therefore dedicates his whole self to the task of
helping others. His is a high character, indeed, his is the embodiment of the teachings of
prophets and sages, the ideal of the Holy Scriptures, the aspiration of humanity.

We are, in truth, the architects and builders
of our character. And in the building of it
every step is vital, every act counts, every
word, every gesture, every move, is significant.
An unkind word, a wrong act, a selfish move,
will, in the end, work more harm to ourselves
than to others. Whatever we say and whatever we do makes a deep reflex impression
upon our own inner being—an impression
which is more lasting than that which we make
upon others. Our conduct is, at first, the result of our choice; that is, many ways are
open to us, we are capable of a variety of
reactions, it is in our power to make any decision, to pursue any course of action. Before
we have actually acted, before we have actually

spoken, before we have opened a channel from our inner being into the outer world, we are still in a potential state, capable of any reaction; but after we have acted, after we have spoken, our state of consciousness centers itself more and more around this outlet which we have made, and we become prone to act again, to speak again, to conduct ourselves again in the same manner. Therefore, the expression of our inner self must be carefully weighed and balanced. It is vain to console ourselves with the thought that a doubtful or indiscreet act today may be followed by better conduct on the morrow. One indiscretion will only invite another indiscretion, just as one act of kindness or courtesy will lead to other kindred acts of fineness.

A good character, because of its deep, spiritual significance, carries with it a profound practical message, for everything that is spiritual must necessarily, as we have shown in Jewish Science, be also practical in its appeal. A good character is not only vital, for example, in human fellowship, but it is also essential in business relationship. A good character is the basis of trust, it is the chief security for credit, it is the foundation of confidence and reliability. Everyone believes in good character, but there are many who draw a line of demarcation between conduct in social relations, and conduct in business. They admit, they profess, in fact, that good character is vital to society, but they maintain that the standards advocated in human fellowship at large cannot be applied to business. They tell us that *business is business;* by this they mean to imply that business has its own standards, that it follows methods distinctly its own, that it cannot possibly adopt the ethics of idealists and still be successful, that it is therefore compelled to make deviations from the practices which constitute high character. We say to these men that this is not at all the case. Character in business is by far a greater asset than energy, than effort, than ambition, than great material resources, than all of these combined. When those who deal with you know that your intentions are always genuine, that your claims are always true, that your word is sacred, that you are thoughtful of others' interests as well as of your own, then you may be assured that success will be yours. People appreciate those whom they can trust, they seek out those over whose word there is not a shadow of doubt, they love to have their dealings with those who have convinced them of their integrity and uprightness. Even those very same people who maintain that business is business and that everything within the bounds of the literal word of the legal law is permissible in business, even these seek out reliable men to deal with, and so does the rest of the world. Some *may* succeed through deception and corruption, but their success is for but a moment, it is transient; for mankind has keen eyes and sharp ears and penetrating judgment, and it never fails, in good time, to discriminate between truth and falsehood, or between integrity and dishonesty.

Character is a gift greater than any other that one may possess. It is greater than intellect, for intellect is only a lense of vision with which to penetrate into the depths of the world; but intellect alone does not give us a sympathetic outlook on life, it does not unite us with our fellowmen. Character is greater than knowledge, for knowledge is only the accumulated grasp of things, it is the harvest of the efforts of the intellect; but knowledge alone does not enhance human life, it does not bring man nearer to his neighbor, it does not of itself augment human happiness. But where these gifts fall short, character shows itself supreme. For nobility of character breeds sympathy, it generates fellowship, it multiplies love, it increases human happiness.